CHRISTIANS AT WORK IN A HURTING WORLD

Though this book is designed for group study, it is also intended for your personal enjoyment and spiritual growth. A leader's guide is available from your local bookstore or from your publisher.

Copyright 1990
Beacon Hill Press of Kansas City
Kansas City, Missouri

Printed in the United States of America

ISBN: 083-411-2698

Editor
Stephen M. Miller

Editorial Assistant
Kathryn Roblee

Editorial Committee
Stephen M. Miller
Carl Pierce
Dan Riemenschneider
Gene Van Note
Lyle Williams
Aron Willis

Photo Credits

Cover photo by William Viggiano. A homeless mother and child sleeping at sunup, a few blocks from the Hudson River, in West Greenwich Village, New York City. With soaring rents and high security deposits, parents sometimes must choose between food for their children or a roof over their head. Viggiano says he has been photographing the homeless for over a decade, but only in recent years has he seen whole families on the streets.

5, Strix Pix; 11, © 1990, Cleo Freelance Photo; 22, Eugene Harris; 31, 59, 68, 116 © 1990, Luke Golobitsh; 42, © 1990, Jim West; 52, © 1989 by Jeffrey High, Image Productions; 82, Media International; 90, © 1990, Alan Oddie, Photo Edit; 99, © 1990, William B. Pope; 107, © 1990, Jean-Claude Lejeune.

Bible Credits

Unless otherwise indicated, all Scripture references are from *The Holy Bible, New International Version,* copyright © 1973, 1978, 1984 by the International Bible Society, and are used by permission.

Contents

Chapter 1 **Video Seduction** 5
An Anonymous Writer

Chapter 2 **The Problem of Christians in Politics** 11
Charles Colson

Chapter 3 **The Story of One Homeless Man** 22
Dean Nelson

Chapter 4 **You Know You're Prejudiced When** ...31
Dwight T. Gregory

Chapter 5 **The Convenient Abortion for Desperate Times** 42
Jean Purcell

Chapter 6 **Single Parents in Search of Help**......52
David Lambert

Chapter 7 **When We're Not Sure It's Child Abuse** 59
Scott Skiles

Chapter 8 **What Kind of Man Would Beat His Wife?** 68
Kay Marshall Strom

Chapter 9 **Simple Living: From Barbecued Rat to $700 Million for Chewing Gum** 82
Larry Dinkins

Chapter 10 **How Churches Can Fight Drug Abuse** 90
Jerry Hull

Chapter 11 **What Churches Are Doing (or Could Be Doing) for the Disabled**..99
Dorothy I. Baird

Chapter 12 **The Graying of the Church** 107
Tim Stafford

Chapter 13 **Building Bridges to Your Neighbors**..116
Tom Eisenman

Chapter 1

Video Seduction

by An Anonymous Writer

Background Scripture: Psalm 97:10, Philippians 4:8; James 1:13-15; 1 John 1:9

MY ACTIONS seemed so out of character for a Christian leader, an ordained minister. What had happened in my mind and conscience? I thought. How had Satan's fiery darts penetrated so deeply?

It all started so innocently. The video cassette recorder was a gift to enhance my ministry. Many of my friends use VCRs to view messages by speakers such as James Dobson and Charles Swindoll. Animated Bible stories for children are available on videotape. Seminaries offer videotaped classes for off-campus students.

My friends also use video equipment to record television programs missed because of ministry commitments and to enjoy an occasional Hollywood film. Many believers are also renting movies from video rental shops. This is where my temptation began. I discovered that thousands of titles are available for cheap rental, sometimes for as little as a dollar an evening.

During the first months of use, my family and I viewed several Walt Disney classics—*Mary Poppins, Swiss Family Robinson,* and *Pete's Dragon.* But as I selected our family movies at the local video shop, an exciting selection of fast-action adventure movies caught my eye. As I browsed these titles, I recognized that most were unsuitable for family viewing. But they didn't seem to be "bad" movies and had entertainment promise. When I began to hear Christian friends talking about many of these movies, I justified viewing less-than-wholesome entertainment: "Others are doing it."

And so I would select a family movie and one of a more mature theme for my wife and me to watch after the children were in bed.

I enjoyed the action in these films, but I was also troubled. The actors used profanity. The women often wore skimpy attire. More often than not there were scenes portraying violence and sexual immorality. I tolerated these portions because the films were 90 percent wholesome entertainment.

Before long, however, I found the sexual scenes more enticing and less offensive.

My son once noticed the extra movie and asked if he

could see it, too. I explained that it wasn't a movie for kids because it had some bad language and things that were not very nice.

"Then why are you watching it, Dad?" he asked. I had nothing to say in reply.

Most of the movies I viewed with my wife were rated PG (parental guidance). I had yet to rent an R-rated movie (restricted to 18 and older). But a day came that I did. I was attracted by the title and the suggestive picture. I told myself that sex was not the attraction.

Before I realized it, I was watching a movie a weekend—sometimes two. I found myself less interested in reading. I would pick up a book and page through it, but what I really wanted to see was another movie. And there were several titles I couldn't wait to see. So came the midweek movie.

During my video seduction, I experienced a perplexing spiritual struggle. I rationalized viewing discrete sex and partial nudity. I'm mature enough to handle this, I thought. There's nothing wrong with merely viewing these things. I'm not the one doing them.

Yet deep within my heart, I knew I was guilty.

It was especially difficult to carry out an effective ministry during this time. Although I continued my personal devotions out of habit, I knew that my reading of Scripture and prayer was a sham. My enthusiasm for teaching and preaching the Bible waned. I lost boldness in speaking on biblical commands against sexual immorality.

On several occasions I determined that I would not view another R-rated movie. I didn't like the profanity. The stories were inane, never providing the satisfying entertainment I had anticipated. But then, while browsing the shelves in the video shop, looking for a better movie, my flesh would be aroused by sensuous titles.

Video was becoming a necessary element of my life. I looked forward to the midweek movie as a chance to "put my mind in neutral" and relax after a busy day. When my wife was busy with housework or her Bible study, I watched the movie alone, often selecting a more sexually suggestive title.

Still, her moral sensitivity and presence in the home prevented me from viewing some of the more sexually explicit movies I had noticed in the video shops. Then came a weekend when she was to be away at a women's conference. I had not dared to bring an X-rated film home for us to view together, but now was my chance to view one alone.

I contemplated this decision for at least a week. I did not want to give in to this temptation. Yet I could not seem to get the film out of my mind.

On Saturday night I went to the video shop intending to get a family movie. But as I laid a few dollars on the counter for an X-rated movie, I told myself, "It's just curiosity, not lust. Perhaps as a Christian leader I should be aware of what the world is consuming."

What I saw was ugly. The film degraded men and women. The beauty of human sexuality as God designed it and as I had experienced it in marriage was absent. I felt empty, cheated, and defeated.

It was at that point that God brought me to my senses. He had been calling me to repentance all along, but I had been ignoring Him. Shocked by my failure, I realized I was in danger of destroying my life and my ministry. If I hardened my heart and harbored this sin, what would entice me next?

I did four things that night before going to bed. First, I destroyed the identification cards that video shops require when renting tapes. Second, I wrote a letter to my wife, confessing my failure and asking her to pray for my spiritual recovery. Third, I confessed my sin to the Lord and accepted His cleansing. Fourth, I made a decision before God to stay out of video shops.

Later, I took another step. I made myself accountable to a friend—a pastor I greatly respect. I confessed my sin and asked for his prayers, and I promised to let him know if I sensed I was slipping. We agreed to ask each other regularly about our spiritual lives.

I'm writing this not to provide a catharsis for my soul, for I'm assured of God's forgiveness (1 John 1:9), but to warn other Christians who own video equipment. No Christian is immune to the temptations of video seduction.

I would like to share some steps I have taken to avoid the misuse of my video recorder:

I have stopped frequenting video shops. Even though I may not intend to rent an R-rated film when I enter the shop, I often come across these items on the shelves. Browsing for movies in secular video shops gives Satan the opportunity to get in some licks. I may escape without renting a compromising film, but I have exposed myself to suggestive titles that may come to mind when my guard is down.

Many Christian bookstores now rent family films. By renting my videos there, I avoid unnecessary temptation.

In the future, if I must rent from a secular video shop, I will call ahead to reserve the title I want and pick it up at the counter.

I have stopped watching video movies alone. When I'm planning to watch a video movie, I arrange to watch it with my wife, children, and sometimes another family. This helps me to be more selective in my choice of films.

I have limited my video viewing. Leisure and entertainment have their place, but I often gravitate to extremes: "If watching one video a month is enjoyable, one a week will be even more so."

In my opinion, very few secular films are worth spending two hours to watch. The quality diminishes greatly as I move from Academy Award material to low-budget productions. I have decided to save my viewing time for the few high-quality films that are released yearly. I use other leisure time for reading, games, and more interactive recreation.

I'm cultivating opportunities to use my video equipment for ministry. Hundreds of evangelical films are available on videotape, including James Dobson's "Focus on the Family" and "The Kingdom of the Cults" with Walter Martin. My wife and I watched a series on the family by John MacArthur. We are looking for occasions when we can share such materials with a friend or family.

I'm seeking to cultivate God's attitude toward things I view on video. Proverbs 6:16-19 lists the kinds of evil that God hates—lies, bloodshed, and wicked plans. These very evils are emphasized and exalted by the film industry. It's sad to say that I have sometimes been entertained by activities the Lord hates. Solomon reminds me that "to fear the Lord is to hate evil" (Proverbs 8:13). And the Psalmist advises us, "Let those who love the Lord hate evil" (Psalm 97:10).

I'm limiting my viewing to films that meet the criteria of Philippians 4:8. Paul writes, "Finally, brothers, whatever is true, whatever is noble, whatever is right, whatever is pure, whatever is lovely, whatever is admirable—if anything is excellent or praiseworthy—think about such things." If my video viewing meets this standard, it's not likely that my entertainment is dishonoring the Lord.

I forget many things—phone numbers, names, Scripture references—but many explicit and violent scenes of R-rated movies still remain in my mind. I now want to protect my mind from the stain of corruption.

Originally published in *Moody Monthly* magazine, May 1987. Reprinted by permission.

Chapter 2

The Problem
of Christians in Politics

by Charles Colson

*Background Scripture: Joshua 2:1-7; Hebrews 11:30-31;
1 Peter 2:13-17*

CHRISTIANS may well face more problems than others when they become involved in the political process.

For example, at times national security may require not

only concealing the truth, but lying. When I was in the White House, we went to elaborate lengths to conceal essential secret negotiations. Secretary of State Henry Kissinger had a bad cold when he visited Pakistan in 1971—or so we told the press. Actually he had been flown to Bejing to conduct sensitive meetings in preparation for Mr. Nixon's historic visit to China.

Or take the day Nixon announced a major troop withdrawal in Vietnam. He immediately ordered Kissinger to bring the Soviet ambassador to a secret meeting room in the White House basement. "Henry," he roared, "You shake him up. Tell him not to believe these news stories. We're only pulling out a few troops—and if the Russians don't back off in sending supplies to Hanoi, we'll bomb the daylights out of that city. Tell him the president is uncontrollable, a madman—that he'll do anything. Let's keep them off balance." That such meetings took place was flatly denied in order to protect the lives of the withdrawing troops.

Ronald Reagan did the same thing in 1983. When reporters asked about a rumored invasion of Grenada, official White House spokesmen dismissed such questions as "preposterous." Actually, troops were at that moment disembarking on the island's beaches. A "no comment" to the press, however, would have been tantamount to a "yes"—an admission that would have endangered lives.

In these days of delicate international tensions and the instant communications ability of an almost omnipresent press, such deceit is a common instrument of foreign policy. The press even accepts it. In a *Newsweek* interview, crack ABC interviewer Ted Koppel acknowledged that government officials must be "prepared to mislead and ... sometimes even to lie."[1]

Deliberate lies, the corruption of power, compromise with ideological opponents, temptations on all sides—these appear to be the mechanisms of modern government.

Should the Christian avoid the messy business of politics altogether?

The answer must be an emphatic no. There are at least three compelling reasons Christians must be involved in politics.

First, as citizens of the nation or state, Christians have the same civic duties all citizens have: to serve on juries, to pay taxes, to vote, to support candidates they think are best qualified. They are commanded to pray for and respect governing authorities.

Second, as citizens of the kingdom of God they are to bring God's standards of righteousness and justice to bear on the kingdoms of this world. As former Michigan state senator and college professor Stephen Monsma says, Christian political involvement has the "potential to move the political system away from ... the brokering of the self-interest of powerful persons and groups into a renewed concern for the public interest."[2]

Third, Christians have an obligation to bring moral values into the public debate. All law implicitly involves morality; the popular idea that "you can't legislate morality" is a myth. Morality is legislated every day from the vantage point of one value system or another. The question is not whether we will legislate morality, but whose morality will we legislate.

Law is but a body of rules regulating human behavior; it establishes, from the view of the state, the rightness or wrongness of human behavior. Most laws, therefore, have moral implications. Statutes prohibiting murder, mandates for seat belts, or regulations for industrial safety are all designed to protect human life—a reflection of the particular moral view that values the dignity and worth of human life.

The real issue for Christians is not whether they should be involved in politics or contend for laws that affect moral behavior. The question is how.

What Christian Citizens Can Do

On an individual level, political involvement for the Christian entails not only voting and other basic responsibilities of citizenship but dealing directly with political issues, particularly where justice and human dignity are at stake. A friend of mine, a prominent attorney in Ecuador, experienced this firsthand.

Dr. Jorge Crespo was an attorney for labor unions, fighting for justice and humane working conditions for Ecuador's laborers. After meeting with Prison Fellowship's South American regional director, he agreed to consider prison ministry, even though he had always seen prisons as places where delinquents—and some clients—ended up.

As soon as Dr. Crespo walked the cellblocks of a Quito prison, he felt "a deep sensation of pain, something like an echo of the pain of the prisoners. Since we are made in His image, we have been given His compassion toward our neighbor," he explained.

So Dr. Crespo became president of Prison Fellowship Ecuador. As he investigated prison conditions, he uncovered, to his horror, instances of cruelty, deprivation, and misery. In one prison 20 prisoners were wedged into a cell the size of a small bedroom. In another inmates received less care than animals; their food budget was less than that of the officers' guard dogs. In most women's prisons, children were incarcerated along with their mothers. In some cases they were being used as pawns in child prostitution rings to make profits for their parents, the prison guards, or both.

Dr. Crespo and his colleagues documented their case, then began to educate the public through press, radio, and television. They sent letters to the prison wardens with copies to the minister of government; they met with ministers of social rehabilitation and justice. Their campaign was not without personal sacrifice and political risk.

Finally, they approached the tribunal safeguarding Ecuador's provisions for human rights.

Crespo spent two hours testifying about the despicable prison conditions as well as the inhumane treatment of inmates and those who had been detained for crimes but not yet proven guilty.

The justices were shocked. Never before had such ugly topics been addressed in their ornate chambers. At the conclusion, the vice president leaned forward to Dr. Crespo. "You have come here as Christians," he said, "and what you have done today is truly Christian."

As a result of Dr. Crespo's boldness, a series of reforms have been adopted in Ecuador. He has also organized a group of Christian police officers who are working to assure humane police investigation that does not rely on brutality.

Dr. Crespo is seeing slow but deliberate progress in the prisons.

The political and personal risks have been worth it, he says. "To act as Christians we have to stand against injustice, and with prophetic voice talk courageously about truth, justice, fear, love. We ought not to bear infamy or atrocities. I believe a Christian who will remain silent is not a Christian."

Christians like Jorge Crespo who work as private citizens to address problems within the structures of government do so, as Stephen Monsma has written, "not as moral busybodies who are seeking to foist their morals onto all of society by the force of law, but as those who have a passion for justice, as those who respect all persons as unique image bearers of God and who therefore seek to treat them with justice."[3]

What Christian Politicians Can Do

But many others are called to make a Christian witness from positions within government itself. After all, as men like William Wilberforce or the great 19th-century social reformer, Lord Shaftesbury, clearly illustrate, Christians who are politicians can bear a biblical witness on political structures, just as they do in medicine, law, business, labor, education, the arts, or any other walk of life. They exhibit this in their moral witness and their willingness to stand up for unpopular causes, even if such causes benefit society more than their own political careers.

U.S. Senators Sam Nunn of Georgia and William Armstrong of Colorado attended a Bible study several years ago on the topic of restitution as a biblical means of punishment. The two leaders later examined the federal statutes and discovered that restitution was only vaguely mentioned. Even though "lock 'em up" legislation was in political vogue, the two men, both committed Christians, sponsored legislation to set new standards for sentencing: prison for dangerous offenders, but tax-dollar-saving alternative punishments, such as work and restitution programs, for nondangerous offenders. In 1983 the bill was adopted, after heated debate, as a resolution of the Congress and later was used as model legislation by several states.

Christians can also bring mercy, compassion, and friendship to those in the cutthroat business of politics.

After his resignation Mr. Nixon withdrew to isolation behind the walls of his San Clemente compound. For nearly a year, as he struggled to recover from both the deep emotional wounds of Watergate and life-threatening phlebitis, Mr. Nixon saw only his family and a few close friends. No one, other than gloating reporters, tried to visit him.

No one, that is, except one man who had opposed Mr. Nixon as vigorously as anyone in the senate. Without fanfare, Mark Hatfield, an evangelical Christian, traveled twice to San Clemente. His reason? Simply, as he told me later, "to let Mr. Nixon know that someone loved him."

Sometimes even minor things can have a significant ripple effect in the everyday business of government. Concerned about the pressures government service puts on congressional families, Congressmen Frank Wolf and Dan Coates hosted a series of receptions to show James Dobson's excellent family-counseling films. More than a hundred members and their spouses attended; several later sought counseling help. Through Coates and Wolf the films were also shown to the joint chiefs of staff and Pentagon officials, who have since made them available for use in military training programs.

Christians in public office are motivated by something more than popularity or self-interest, something that frees them from being held hostage to political expediency. Their motivation to pursue what is right, in obedience to God, also gives them a source of wisdom and confidence beyond their own abilities.

But Christians are exposed to great struggles of conscience. They are honor bound to be the best statesmen they can be, as well as the best Christians they can be. These competing allegiances caused British writer Harry Blamires to conclude that perhaps "a good Christian [can] be a good politician ... but it is probably quite impossible for a good Christian to be a highly successful politician."[4]

Blamires may well have been referring to the issue of divided allegiances between God and the state. When there is a conflict of loyalty, the sincere Christian must obey God. Yet the politician's oath of office is to uphold the laws of the state.

The prevailing American view that faith is something private with no effect on public responsibility was first put forth by John Kennedy in a dramatic speech to the Houston Ministerial Association in the 1960 campaign. Protestants feared that Kennedy, a Catholic, would be bound by the dictates of the Roman church. So Kennedy pulled off a political masterstroke when he told the Texas ministers, mostly Baptists, that "whatever issue may come before me as president, if I'm elected ... I will make my decision in accordance ...

with what my conscience tells me to be in the national interest, and without regard to outside religious pressure or dictate. And no power or threat of punishment could cause me to decide otherwise."[5]

Kennedy's message, which brought the house down, was a key to his election. But it set a precedent that has now become part of established American political wisdom: One's religious convictions must have no effect on one's public decisions.

But consider Kennedy's words: "No power ... could cause me to decide otherwise." Not God? Though Kennedy's approach was enormously popular, it was also a renunciation of any influence his religion might have. He put his church responsibility under his patriotism—or his candidacy.

By contrast, Hilaire Belloc stood for election in 1906 in the British Parliament. As a Roman Catholic, he knew he would have to struggle to overcome religious prejudices, so he decided to confront the issue head-on. In his first campaign speech, he stood at the rostrum with a rosary in his hand and said, "I am a Catholic. As far as possible I go to Mass every day. As far as possible I kneel down and tell these beads every day. If you reject me on account of my religion, I shall thank God that He has spared me the indignity of being your representative."[6] He was elected.

Some conclude, however, that the officeholder in a free society cannot *impose* personal views on the electorate; the democratic process must be respected. That is true.

And they go on to conclude that the Christian officeholder is thus free, in the name of political prudence, to support or accept the majority will when it is contrary to Christian teaching (a view eloquently espoused by New York Governor Mario Cuomo in his 1984 Notre Dame address). Religious conviction is thereby reduced to a private matter; the social implications of the gospel are simply ignored.

Another position, often taken in reaction to the

Kennedy-Cuomo view, is represented by those who are prepared to thrust their own theological view on an unsuspecting nation. This view, expressed by some in political debate today, argues that a Christian politician should use his position to speak for God.

Both views—privatized faith and using political power to play God—are deeply flawed. This brings us full circle: Is it possible for a devout Christian to serve in public office without compromising either his conscience or constituency?

It is possible. But only if the Christian officeholder understands several key truths.

First, a government official must not play God; one's duty is to help preserve order and justice, not to use government to accomplish the goals of the church.

Second, the Christian must respect the rights of all religious groups and insure that government protects every citizen's freedom of conscience.

A third concern brings us back to the question posed at the outset of this chapter. What about the Christian responsibility in situations where national leaders cannot be entirely candid in public pronouncements? Consider the dilemma posed by the Reagan administration's disinformation campaign designed to unsettle the government of Mohammar Khadaffi—a murderous tyrant who imperiled any number of nations. Confronted with this question, Secretary of State George Shultz defended the government's actions by quoting Winston Churchill: "In times of war, the truth is so precious, it must be attended by a bodyguard of lies."

The pressures of nuclear-age diplomacy create conscience-wrenching agony for sincere Christians in office. Yet the Bible offers some surprising principles, citing Rahab, a prostitute, as one of the great heroes of the faith. Why? Rahab's place in history was established by the fact that she lied to protect Hebrew spies. Similarly, concentration-camp survivor Corrie ten Boom lied to the Nazis to protect the Jews she was hiding. Most Christians today would likely do the same for, in this cruel and complex world, a lesser evil may be required to prevent a greater one. A Christian in public office may be placed in a similar situation, say, to save the lives of hostages. If the situation forced the Christian to lie against his conscience, the Christian should resign.

Our Duty as Christians

Within these limits, then, we can conclude that Christians have a duty, for the good of society as a whole, to bring the values of the kingdom of God to bear within the kingdoms of humanity.

It is fair to say, however, that Christians have not done a particularly good job at this task. Often they have terrified their secular neighbors, who see Christian political activists as either backwoods bigots or religious ayatollahs attempting to assault them with Bible verses or religious rules. It is not only wrong but unwise for Christians to shake their Bible and arrogantly assert that "God says . . ." That is the quickest way for Christians, a distinct minority in civil affairs, to lose their case altogether.

Instead, positions should be argued on their merits. If the case is sound, a majority can be persuaded; that's the way democracies and free nations are supposed to work.

I'm often asked to meet with government officials concerned with criminal justice policies. They are frustrated. The more prisons are built—at great expense—the more the crime rate goes up. So whenever I suggest restitution as an inexpensive and effective alternative to prison for nonviolent offenders, politicians are receptive. But only after I have cited the facts of the position do I explain that the source of restitution was God's law prescribed to Moses at Sinai.[7]

Christians are to do their duty as best they can. But

even when they feel that they are making no difference, that they are failing to bring Christian values to the public arena, success is not the criteria. Faithfulness is. For in the end, Christians have the assurance that even the most difficult political situations are in the hands of a sovereign God.

---

1. "America's Question and Answer Man," *Newsweek* (June 15, 1987), 56.

2. Stephen Monsma, "The Promises and Pitfalls of Evangelical Political Involvement," a speech (October 17, 1986), 9.

3. Monsma, 15-16.

4. Harry Blamires, *The Christian Mind* (London: S.P.C.K, 1963), 25.

5. Vernon Grounds, "Crosscurrents," *Moody Monthly* (July/August 1986), 80.

6. From *The Little, Brown Book of Anecdotes* (Boston: Little, Brown, 1985), 50.

7. Exodus 21—22.

Excerpt from *Kingdoms in Conflict,* by Charles Colson. Copyright © 1987 by Charles Colson. Reprinted by permission of William Morrow and Company, Inc.

Chapter 3

A homeless person sleeps on Ocean Beach, in San Diego.

The Story of One Homeless Man

by Dean Nelson

Background Scripture: Matthew 25:31-46

THE WORD IS OUT. At the doughnut shop on University Avenue in San Diego, the management won't hassle you if you're a street person.

They'll give you coffee refills and let you sit inside for a long time if you don't get too loud or abusive. It's not a particularly clean place, but it has light and a roof. So it does the job.

I recently walked in there late one Friday afternoon. Through an acquaintance I had arranged to interview a man who had lived on the streets for years—under bridges, in canyons, in a car. He suggested we meet in the doughnut shop.

Inside I saw only two customers. One was a clean-shaven, fit-looking gentleman working a crossword puzzle book, and the other was a true down-and-outer staring out the window.

I headed for the oblivious latter but was interrupted by the man working the puzzle.

"Mr. Nelson? I'm Rick."*

In that moment a stereotype died. I had prepared myself for a repeat of my high school experience as an orderly in the emergency room of Hennepin County General Hospital in Minneapolis. I saw many homeless there. Part of my job was to bathe, restrain, and calm the homeless who came in. My assessment was that these people were dirty, drunk, dangerous, and dumb.

But Rick was alarmingly articulate. His use of the language showed me he was no vegetable.

He told me about moving to San Diego after spending 15 years in a Georgia prison, beginning at age 14. After his money ran out, he couldn't pay the $30.00 a week for his room in a downtown hotel. He was evicted, so he spent some nights on the couch in a friend's living room.

"She came home from work at 1 A.M., flew into a rage, and threw me out. That was the first night I spent outside in a park. The next day I decided that if this was the way it was going to be, I needed to find out how to do this from the people who know."

The squatter's camp he tried downtown under a freeway overpass was too dangerous, he decided. Too many muggings, too many police raids, too many risks.

"My vulnerability was plain to me," he said. "Once you're asleep, anything can happen. I can survive a beating, but not a stabbing or shooting. I knew I had to get away from downtown, even though that's where the food lines were. I looked around until I found an ideal spot."

The spot was in a canyon in a residential area called Golden Hill. He took a box spring someone had thrown into the canyon, collected some blankets from dumps, and built a camouflaged shelter in the bushes. After the first rain, he found some plastic sheeting in a furniture store dumpster.

"I never told anyone about it, and I never went there during the day," he said. He lived there for a year and a half, using public rest rooms to shave and wash. He said he wanted to keep clean and shaved because if he lost that discipline, he feared it would be too difficult to get it back. Keeping clean remained one of his few links to civilization.

Eventually, some kids exploring in the canyon found his home and ransacked it.

"I figured they were telling me to get out," he said. Then it was back to the street.

Trapped People, Trapped Whales

One of the most devastating editorial cartoons of 1988 was Jeff Danziger's in the *Christian Science Monitor.* Danziger drew the cartoon during the much-celebrated liberation of two whales trapped in ice off the Alaskan coast. The nation, well-rehearsed after the 1987 rescue of Jessica McLure from a backyard well in Texas, knew how to gear up for trapped, helpless creatures. On behalf of the two stranded whales, news crews mobilized, companies donated products, people poured in money, entrepreneurs offered solutions, and ships steamed in to break up the ice.

Phil Donahue, Oprah Winfrey, Ted Koppel all got in the act. I was hoping Geraldo Rivera would don a sealskin suit and dive in the icy water to show us how hard it is to breathe when you can't come up for air. But he didn't.

During the hoopla, Danziger drew a cartoon of two homeless people freezing on a park bench. The caption: Two mammals who had the misfortune not to be born whales.

I have to admit the whale rescue was thrilling to watch. It had the ending of a Walt Disney fairy tale, and we could cheer for all the heroes. Cue the orchestra and roll the credits.

Poor people in our society don't fit in the fairy tale plot, though. So it's harder to get excited about them. It isn't a matter of just cutting enough air holes for them until they can get out into the open water. They'll always be with us. The problem is permanent.

It has become trendy, though, to talk about the homeless. On the November 1988 California ballot was a measure to create a state bureau to deal with hunger and homelessness. It was defeated largely because voters weren't convinced that another layer of bureaucracy was the answer.

Meanwhile, some cities in the Southwest are trying to play down their area's mild climate so homeless people won't be drawn there. To discourage the homeless already there, city governments have started seizing belongings of transients and throwing them in the trash.

In a similar measure, San Francisco recently banned free food distribution in Golden Gate Park. The distributors lacked official permits, and besides, they were attracting undesirables. These nasty things aren't limited to just the Southwest, though. Remember New York City's attempt to round up street people and commit them to mental institutions?

On the positive side, the Houston school district opens its gymnasium at night during the winter to provide shelter for homeless children.

We're at the point where we can no longer ignore the homeless. There are too many of them. Their problems are too severe. Air holes aren't enough.

Government has tried to be the answer. In my view, Lyndon Johnson's Great Society was a great theory. I really wish it would have worked. Administration after administration has shown us, though, that giving away money is not an effective way to deal with poverty. A policy of ignoring the problem doesn't work either, as we have seen from recent administrations.

Homelessness: The Addiction

In the view of my new friend Rick, the problem is compounded by what happens to a person once he is on the street for a while.

"You eventually just accept your way of life," he said. "After spending a year in the canyon, it became a very easy way to live. There are no responsibilities, no status to uphold. I could sleep when I wanted, drink when I wanted. You don't have to be at any place at any certain time. You stop thinking about living another way. That's not to say I was satisfied with where I was. I was striving to change my situation. I felt the toll of the street people. I got aggressive, angry, distraught, and thought, What's the use?

"But bit by bit, day by day, you get addicted. Social services become addictive after a while, too. You get your money, and nobody is looking over your shoulder.

"You don't have a place to clean up in, you don't have a home, you just assume that a job is just as impossible. You just stop considering the possibility."

Regarding the specific problem of hunger, the only agricultural system that worked to my knowledge was the biblical one that allowed the poor to have what was left after the harvest. It didn't cure poverty, but it provided meals.

What Christians Are Doing

Churches from many denominations are doing that today—providing meals. My own denomination, the Church of the Nazarene, has celebrated examples like the Lamb's Club in Manhattan, Golden Gate Ministries in San Francisco, the Community of Hope in Washington, D.C., and other efforts sponsored by local congregations.

San Diego First Church of the Nazarene, where I attend, does what a lot of churches could do. The congregation works with First Baptist Church in Ocean Beach and provides meals once a week for the street people and activities for their children. Ocean Beach is where many homeless people stay. Ocean Beach, some say, is where the debris meets the sea.

Our church board has even given approval for the pastors to spend what they think is necessary to help people they meet. Sometimes that means a plane ticket for a runaway to go back home.

Father Joe Carroll is a local hero for aggressively providing food and shelter for the San Diego poor, at the St. Vincent de Paul Center downtown. Father Bruce Ritter and the Covenant House in New York are nationally known for work with children. Father Ritter's book *Sometimes God Has a Child's Face* is both thrilling and devastating.

Habitat for Humanity has helped the poor build and own their own houses. The Struve Clinic in Minneapolis provides low-cost health care to the poor. Doctors and nurses forego higher paying jobs so they can work among Native Americans, and the facilities are often in churches.

But is that all we should do for the poor—give away food, shelter, plane tickets, and advice?

At the turn of the century, Phineas F. Bresee made it clear when he helped begin the Church of the Nazarene that the denomination's emphasis should be on taking the gospel to the poor. A century and a half before, John Wesley took the gospel to the poor of England. For both Bresee and Wesley, the gospel, by the way, included food and shelter.

"People need something to believe in if they are going to change," Rick told me. "But it's hard to give people something to believe when they need something to eat or drink."

Most church soup kitchens he went to made the crowd listen to a sermon before the meal was served.

"I don't believe in force feeding people," he said. "An hour is a long time to sit when all you can think about is your stomach, a drink, or some drugs. It would be more meaningful if the time was informative. Get a guy up there who has overcome obstacles and who encourages them to make the best of their situation. Someone who can show me that my case is not hopeless. Most street people scorn the idea of church, but they go there to get fed."

In his opinion, churches should concentrate their efforts on those who aren't yet hard-core street people.

"If you can curtail those who aren't yet there, you can keep the numbers from growing," he said. "The hard-core need professional help and must be put in a controlled environment."

Mother Teresa made a comment about poverty that hasn't yet let go of me. I'm paraphrasing, but she said we owe a great debt of gratitude to the poor. Did you catch that? The poor don't owe us for food and shelter but we owe them. We owe them because they give us the opportunity to be Jesus and to minister to Jesus who comes to us as a poor, hungry, naked, diseased person.

I don't believe she's talking about some symbolic Jesus here. She's talking about the real Jesus. And she's talking about our own need to accept some level of poverty—spiritually and otherwise.

Henri Nouwen, in his book *Reaching Out,* says, and I'm paraphrasing again, poverty is a good host. The less you have, the more willing you are to share. The more you have, the tighter you hold on, and build fences around, and hire security guards to protect.

A thought: Could that bolted door philosophy apply to some churches and their relationship with the poor?

An illustration: San Diego First Church used to meet in a gymnasium. It was temporary, until a new place could be built. Lots of people hated that gym. The stairs were too steep. It got too noisy. To many, there was something offensive about worshiping between basketball hoops. Some people stopped coming because of it. You know what it means when people stop coming. They stop giving. But several people from the streets, caves, and doorways of Ocean Beach came. They were the ones we fed on Monday nights.

Then our new church was completed. Just a few hundred feet away from the gym. It's a beautiful building. We haven't seen any of the Ocean Beach people in it.

A speculation: The apparent wealth attached to that building either made them uncomfortable in it, or the niceness of it made us uncomfortable having them in it. No harm could be done in a gym. And do you know what? The worship services in the gym were good ones, just like they are in the new place. Comparative poverty made us better hosts than we are now, I think.

A question: Why haven't the churches opened their doors to house homeless children the way the Houston school district does? I'll bet I know. Somebody mentioned insurance. Licensing. Theft. And forgot to mention Matthew 25.

A Happy Ending for Rick

It looks like Rick is going to make it. He was sitting in that doughnut shop on University Avenue last year when the manager told him one of the employees didn't show up for work. He asked Rick if he wanted a job. The first night he got coffee and doughnuts for his effort. Then it was money.

He has since worked at a service station and is now a security guard. He has a bank account, a truck, and a one-room apartment with a kitchenette and a community bathroom.

"I messed up a lot in my past," he said. "There are a lot of ghosts that still won't let me go. But I've got to make the best out of what I've got left."

He's confident he's left the canyon for good.

---

*Rick is not the man's real name.

Dean Nelson is assistant professor of journalism at Point Loma Nazarene College, San Diego, Calif., and a free-lance writer for the *Boston Globe* and other newspapers and magazines.

Chapter 4

You Know You're Prejudiced When...

by Dwight T. Gregory

Background Scripture: Matthew 7:1-2; 1 Corinthians 6:9-11; Philippians 2:1-8

HEAR THE WORD of the Christians.
"It's impossible to teach colored girls sexual morality."
"I don't want any fried chicken made by white folks. They never clean it enough."

"You shouldn't ever trust an Indian. They always find some way to take advantage of you."

"Koreans aren't honest, even after they're converted."

"I don't mind having them in the school, but I surely wouldn't want my daughter to marry one of them."

"If someone in my family is sick, I always look for a Jewish doctor. They're smarter, you know."

(To a church secretary with a Brooklyn accent) "You don't *sound* like a Christian!"

I didn't make up these quotes. They are deadly mouth-to-ear missiles from the lips of Christians I've known and ministered to. These generic prejudgments reflect a definition of prejudice from a person whose name has been lost to time. This person said, "Prejudice is being down on something you're not up on."

Now hear the word of Jesus.

"Do not judge, or you too will be judged. For in the same way you judge others, you will be judged, and with the measure you use, it will be measured to you" (Matthew 7:1-2).

Why do the words of Christ's followers not reflect the words of Christ? Can a Christian be prejudiced?

If you think prejudice dies at the rebirth of conversion, or is washed away at the heart cleansing of entire sanctification, think again. Prejudice takes time to learn. And it takes time to unlearn.

Sometimes prejudice is bold, brazen, and obvious. But more often it is quiet, subtle, and disguised. If that is so, how can we recognize it?

Prejudice Is Alive and Lurking When...

1. We have a sense of superiority

In my college days, someone told me people of culture ate their beef rare. For a long time it embarrassed me when my family ordered their steaks "well done," although I couldn't manage more than medium.

From childhood we have been trained that our way of eating, talking, dressing, and thinking is "right" or "normal." That's OK to an extent. We need to feel comfortable with ourselves. The danger comes when we conclude other people are "wrong."

2. We have an unfounded fear of others

We can't love anyone we are afraid of.

When I take visitors through the ethnic neighborhoods of New York City, they sometimes ask, "Is it safe?"

I understand their question. They have every right to ask it, for we are all conditioned to fear what is different. It's healthy for us to use caution on unfamiliar turf. But paralyzing fear can blind us to beauty and can block relationships.

If we fear people who are different, we miss opportunities to give—or receive—a measure of God's love.

3. We limit opportunities

Frightening results emerged from a study I read about in which teachers were given false reports about past grades of some students.

Most students the teachers thought were academically weak performed much more poorly in their classes than they had in the past. Researchers concluded these lessened skills had to do with the teachers lessened expectations.

Even when prejudice is not malicious, it is harmful.

4. We horde power and privilege

In the vast majority of companies throughout the United States and Canada, white males of Protestant, Northern European background hold the highest positions. And the percentage of men in these jobs is much higher than the percentage of white males in the general population. In other words, they have more than their share of power.

Men and women of other ethnic groups have been granted certain unwritten franchises. In some East Coast cities, the Irish dominate the police force and the Italians the fruit and vegetable business.

I find it interesting to listen to arguments about opening a particular field to others. A key issue is always the concern about "competence" or "quality." But I can't help wondering if the real, unspoken issue is job security. Do those in power simply want to protect their jobs from other qualified people?

Our job security should come from our competence, not our race.

I heard of two Christian men arguing about prejudice. One said, "I reject the idea of collective guilt. I'm not responsible for the problems just because I'm white. I've never owned a slave. I've never consciously discriminated against anyone. I don't tell ethnic jokes." The other man asked, "Have you rejected any of the privileges that have come to you and been denied to others through decades of discrimination?"

There was a long silence.

According to Philippians 2, the way Jesus saved us was by refusing to cling to power and privileges that came from being equal with God the Father. Perhaps to save others from discrimination we need to release some of the power and privileges that have been handed down to us.

5. We assume people can't change

A friend of mine loves to tell the story of his family's conversion. Some of my friend's distant, Christian relatives prayed regularly for the salvation of the whole extended family—for everyone except my friend's family. It seems they figured my friend's family was beyond hope: gamblers, drug dealers, hard-core troublemakers.

But when one of my friend's drug-dealing brothers was thoroughly saved, it touched off a chain reaction that led to the salvation of 60 relatives. And it started with someone that a few Christians were too prejudiced to pray for.

1 Corinthians 6 includes a long list of sinners who "will not inherit the kingdom of God." The passage goes on to say, "that is what some of you were."

For instance, when we say homosexuals are harder for

God to save than gossips, we raise to life a subtle form of prejudice that stifles prayer and hinders God's work.

6. We treat someone as a "category" rather than a person

My friend, Bob Kaplowitz, has cerebral palsy. He finds it hard to speak clearly. But he has a master's degree in musicology and knows more about the great operas than any other person I know. Anyone who views him simply as a handicapped person will miss the skills, intelligence, and insight he has to offer. Another young woman once told me she had chosen to attend our church because we treated her as a person instead of a "blind person," which she also happened to be.

Every human being has a wealth of experience and wisdom.

Pigeon holes aren't comfortable very long, even for pigeons.

7. Our actions are rooted in revenge

You would think victims of prejudice would be most eager to avoid practicing it. But sin blocks such a rational response.

God had to remind the children of Israel to treat their servants kindly. "Remember that you were slaves in Egypt" (Deuteronomy 15:15). Treating people with respect doesn't come automatically. In fact, for those who have been discriminated against, just the opposite is often true. People who have overcome discrimination and have reached some of their goals may feel bitter about the past and fearful about the future. In their hurting, they may grow to hate:

• Any who remind them of former oppressors. "They're all empty-headed bigots. Who needs them?"

• New climbers at the bottom rung of the ladder. "It feels good to look *down* on someone else for a change."

• Speed climbers who zoom up the ladder without paying their dues. "Our people had to struggle to get where they are. Why should this guy have it so easy?"

As a member of the dominant American culture, I find it hard to understand fully the feelings of prejudice victims. But I came nearest to experiencing these feelings for myself a few years ago when my wife became a victim of "reverse discrimination." Nina had given up her evenings and summers to take classes to prepare for a teaching position she seemed certain to get. But just weeks before school was to start, she got word that the job had gone to someone else, mainly because a racial quota needed filled.

It took months for us to overcome the feelings of betrayal, rejection, and anger. It wasn't easy to see things from the other teacher's point of view.

If nothing else, the experience helped us understand the anger we have seen in others. If one incident could be so disruptive, how about a *lifetime* of rejections because of color or some other unchanging fact of life?

8. We elevate a lesser quality above Christ's work in the heart

Many of us can tell a story of a friend from a Christian family who chose a spouse from the "wrong" racial or ethnic group. As the story often goes, the parents cried, "How could you do this to us?" Sometimes family ties are broken for years.

Isn't it ironic how comparatively little fuss is made in the same family when another brother or sister chooses someone of the right color—but with no profession of faith in Christ? Our prejudices reveal more than we admit about what is really important to us.

How to Overcome Prejudice

Because we learn prejudice from many sources, we have to unlearn it through many strategies.

1. The media

An incredible amount of anti-Black, anti-Jewish, and other "anti" literature is available—all too often in Christian homes. Sometimes this masquerades as serious journalism. Films, plays, and radio talk shows sometimes fan the flames of hatred. People nurtured by "hate" media need to seek out materials that present insights on the other side of the discussion.

Biographies, autobiographies, and novels from groups we have not known well can be helpful. For me, the play and film *A Raisin in the Sun,* and its later musical version *Raisin,* were a powerful and balancing influence. I have watched them, in one form or another, at least six times. Each time they give me a new grasp of the feelings of a Black, urban culture I had no exposure to during my Colorado small-town upbringing. But they also gave me new understanding of myself. More recently, the novels of Chaim Potok have given me a feel for the Jewish experience in America.

2. Relationships

Nothing in literature, however, can substitute for relationships with real people. A white member of a church I pastored in New Jersey once greeted separately two neighbors who had moved onto the block about the same time. One family was Black, the other Puerto Rican. The Black family said they had moved out of New York City to get away from the Puerto Ricans. The Puerto Rican family had moved to get away from the Blacks. Months later, over the coffee table, members from all three families were able to laugh together about their earlier fears and misconceptions.

3. The home

The best time to combat prejudice is before it starts. We can teach our children to enjoy and appreciate people of different backgrounds. The 1950s ideal of being "colorblind" was unrealistic. Children are smart enough to know there are differences in the way people look, talk, and act. There is a fine line between "understanding cultural differences" and unhealthy "stereotyping." The difference is in the attitude. Are we trying to know and love the people better or simply trying to "label" them and go on with our own "normal" life?

In the home, parents must avoid bad examples in vocabulary. Also, children will undoubtedly bring home inappropriate jokes or expressions, and the youngsters must be corrected early so they don't have to be de-programmed later.

News stories about racial conflicts or other incidents give parents a chance to discuss these issues with older children. Young children delight in reading the same books over and over. Parents can see to it that some of their books portray people of different backgrounds in positive ways.

In my family, we chose to live in a racially integrated neighborhood. Not every family has that privilege.

Other small things, such as experimenting with ethic food—Mexican, Chinese (not canned please), or Indian—may help children see that "different" does not necessarily mean "bad." Sometimes the parents need to learn that first.

4. The church

The church should be a major force in the war against prejudice. But its weapons have often grown rusty.

Most churches would consider themselves "open" to all kinds of people. But if sermons include stories about "the old colored preacher" in a patronizing or demeaning way, the barriers are up as clearly as if the guards were at the door.

Thirty years ago the church solution seemed simple: integration. More recent experience has shown that the matter is not so simple.

Experience has shown that churches that clearly target one segment of the population can usually be more effective in ministry. Yet many churches have succeeded in building a very diverse congregation.

Some churches, such as Wesley Chapel Free Methodist in Toronto, and the Jersey City Church of the Nazarene, have different congregations of three or more languages worshiping under the same roof. At Toronto the English congregation includes around 30 nationalities and every shade of color. In a number of these multicultural churches, a key factor has been a pastor with previous overseas missionary experience or special training in cross-cultural communication.

Few congregations will have the opportunity to become so dramatically diverse. What can the more "ordinary" church do to overcome prejudice?

- First, determine to be open to anyone the Lord may send. There is no place in the kingdom of God for churches that willfully exclude anyone because of color, economic level, or past sin.
- Second, consider who is being excluded unintentionally. Make some changes so a broader range of people can feel at home. When the neighborhood starts to change, don't give up on welcoming newcomers.

For the door to be fully open to people in the community, the church must have warm, cultural touches in music or other areas to help most types of people feel at home. As Pastor Bill Leslie of LaSalle Street Church in Chicago has said, "Each person must hear his own sound."

By listening carefully and getting personally acquainted, it is possible for the church to make the necessary changes. Some churches have felt they could make the transition only with the help of an additional pastor of another race or background. But desire and insight are more important than language or skin color.

Don Shoemaker of Jersey City Wesleyan, and the late John Riggs of Los Angeles Second Free Methodist are only two examples of white pastors who have led their churches through a dramatic change in racial composition of the community. In both cases a critical factor was a commitment to long-term ministry in the same church and community. How many more churches might have been successful if they hadn't listened to those who said it couldn't be done?

- Third, recognize the limits. Not every pastor or

church will be as successful as Paul in becoming "all things to all men so that by all possible means I might save some" (1 Corinthians 9:22).

While serving a church in Passaic, N.J., I was proud that our congregation included Black, white, Hispanic, and Chinese members. But when some members brought Japanese neighbors, we found they could relate to some of us one-to-one but were not comfortable in the services. We looked for a Japanese church to refer them to and found none in the area—but nearly 20,000 Japanese people.

Eventually I volunteered to begin a Japanese church there. Over the next six years I had the wonderful privilege of planting a Japanese congregation that is continuing to grow under a new Japanese pastor. Very few of the members would ever have been won to Christ or fully incorporated into church life through our English congregation or any other in the area.

• Fourth, find ways to cooperate with churches of a different style, not only on an annual "Brotherhood Sunday," but regularly. Possibilities include pulpit and choir exchanges, regional youth camps, work projects *together* (not just the privileged majority reaching down to help the poor minorities), and city-wide multicultural services.

One of the highlights of the year for the New York City area Free Methodist churches is the Thanksgiving weekend Praise Rally. People come together to worship God in many languages and styles. (We now have six languages.)

• Finally, challenge individual Christians to overcome their fears and prejudices. We must not be so prejudiced against bigots that we can't disciple them.

In my first pastorate, one of the men who opened his life to Christ seemed to fit the profile of the "redneck." He had a strong case of racial hostility.

Steve told me, "I want to get out of Jersey. There's too many niggers here."

I didn't challenge him directly but waited for the right

opportunity to get him together with Payton, a Black man who had responded to the gospel a few months earlier. Both had the same days off, so I asked them to help me do some work at our conference youth camp. I simply told each of them, "Another friend of mine will come along."

As the two sat in the back seat with my one-year-old son between them on the 100-mile trip, the conversation was guarded. The first day at the camp, we worked a little together, but mostly separately. By the next afternoon, I was surprised to see Payton and Steve out in a boat together on the lake. They had discovered fishing was something they had in common. Steve borrowed a lure from Payton, and quickly lost it in the water. When he said nervously, "I'll buy you a new one," Payton replied, with a twinkle in his eye, "Don't bother. I wouldn't if I lost yours."

On the way home, there were no awkward silences. Both men were full of stories about past exploits, current activities, and spiritual adventure.

After a year or two, Steve moved farther away and didn't get to our church often. But the day I dedicated Payton's first daughter, Steve and his family were in church early. He said, "I came here for Payton. I wouldn't miss this day for anything." At the celebration afterward, Steve ate "soul food" with the family and friends, both Black and white. I rejoiced at playing a tiny part in bridging the gap.

Prejudice is all too easily learned. That's the bad news. You can get it by osmosis—you soak it into your brain just by standing around prejudiced people. But the good news is you can unlearn it. And, as usual, experience is the best teacher.

Dwight T. Gregory is an ordained minister in the Free Methodist church. For 16 years he planted churches in New Jersey: one English-speaking congregation, one Spanish, and one Japanese. He is now superintendent of the New York conference. His wife is an elementary teacher in an inner-city Christian school.

Chapter 5

A pro-choice abortion activist walks the picket line
outside a crisis pregnancy center in Detroit.

The Convenient Abortion for Desperate Times

by Jean Purcell

Background Scripture: Exodus 21:22-23; Psalm 139: 13-16

I'M NOT CERTAIN how I got drawn into the abortion issue. But I do know it all started in the early 1980s, when I recommitted my life to Christ.

What's puzzling is that soon after, the subject of abortion started popping into my mind apparently for no reason. It wasn't a topic among my friends. And I don't remember hearing it discussed at length in church.

Before long, curiosity got the better of me. I found a Right to Life office and asked for information. It was not the words that first struck me. It was the untouched color photographs of aborted fetuses at 10 weeks into the pregnancy.

These vivid photos quickly convinced me that abortion did not remove only a "blob of tissue," as I had heard years before. Nor did it simply "empty the uterus." I saw tiny human bodies chopped up. Arms and legs lay severed from the unborn body.

Insights from a Crisis Pregnancy Center

What I learned so disturbed me that in 1983 I volunteered to work one morning each week as a counselor at a pro-life pregnancy center in our community. I wanted to help women and teenage girls who were trying to cope with crisis pregnancy.

The center was staffed by Christian volunteers. It was funded by donations from individuals. On occasion, a church would send a check. All our services were free. We collected maternity and baby clothes to give to mothers needing them, as well as cribs and other supplies. We helped some mothers find housing when their family or friends turned them out. And if a mother wanted adoption information, we supplied it. All services were free.

Since 1973, when the historic Supreme Court case of *Roe vs. Wade* legalized abortion, some of the volunteers I worked with had been regularly housing, feeding, and caring for pregnant women and new mothers who had nowhere to go.

What drew many women to the center was our free

pregnancy test. Many of the women did not want to be pregnant. Many were unmarried.

As I listened to women and girls with unwanted pregnancies, I realized they knew very little about abortion, except that it was an option. Most knew almost nothing about the developmental stages of life before birth.

Most of them were terrified. I could see it clearly in the quiet ones as well as the outspoken ones. I can't count the number of times I heard a version of, "I have to get an abortion. I can't make it without one." And each time I heard those words, I would pray for insight and the right response.

For years, my ignorance had kept me silently on the fence and uninvolved. And for the pregnant women I was counseling, their ignorance could cost their baby's life. It could also cost them a lifetime of guilt and the inability to ever again conceive a child.

The Convenient Thing to Do

Worldwide there are some 40 million abortions each year. In the United States, we perform more than 1½ million legal abortions every year. About one-fourth of all American pregnancies end this way.

The vast majority of these abortions—about 98 percent—are convenience abortions. That means they are done for reasons other than rape, incest, or to protect the mother's health.

Since the legalization of abortion in 1973, some 22 million unborn children in America have died from convenience abortions. If you could lay this many full-term babies shoulder to shoulder, the line would stretch about 2,000 miles. That's long enough to reach from the northeastern shores of New York City clear into southern California.

Women involved in convenience abortions are those who had been willing participants in the act that caused the pregnancy. For them, abortion becomes a way of sidestepping the consequences of prior choices. Hence the term "convenience abortion."

The problem with this phrase is that "convenience" is a mild-sounding word that does not adequately describe the physical and emotional pain that accompany most abortions. A more appropriate term, I think, would be "desperation abortion."

For me, that better describes the anxiety and often sheer fright I saw on the faces of women in the pregnancy center.

I am convinced that convenience abortions do not grow out of clear thinking. They may appear to be reasoned out, but in fact they are full of confusion, haste, and secrecy. It has been my observation that most women considering these abortions do not want to hear about the alternatives. Also—and this is very important—they are likely to have family members, friends, or doctors who will not give them strong reasons for allowing the pregnancy to continue. And if they have not told anyone of the pregnancy, they assume the worst reactions. They fear, especially, telling their family. They fear the pregnancy. And they fear the unborn child, and how it will change their life. This is why it is so important that they have people to go to who will say, "You have other options, and you do not have to go through this alone."

Legally, any female of any age may have an abortion for any reason during the first trimester—the first three months of the pregnancy (in about a half-dozen states, minors need parental consent). That is what the Supreme Court case *Roe vs. Wade* ruled—no restrictions in the first trimester. It also allowed states to regulate abortions in the second trimester (13-24 weeks). And it allowed states to prohibit abortions when the child is considered viable—when it can live outside the mother. But the determination of when the fetus is viable is left to the attending physician. So states can't ban abortion after a set number of weeks or after it has reached a certain weight.[1]

Roe vs. Wade, then, left the prohibition of late abortions up to the states, and the viability issue up to the doctors. Because of this, and because some states have no laws limiting when abortions can be performed, it would be possible for a woman to get an abortion even in the ninth month if she could find a doctor who would perform it.

The vast majority of abortions, however, take place in the first trimester. According to the National Abortion Federation, 90 percent are done during those first 12 weeks. Nine percent are done in the second trimester, between weeks 13 and 24. Less than 1 percent are done in the third trimester.

In most cases, the mother does not have to inform the child's father or her parents. She does not have to get their approval for an abortion. And, if they know and object, they have no legal right to stop her.

Pro-Choice Arguments, Pro-Life Arguments

In the abortion debate, there are two major camps: pro-choice and pro-life.

Pro-choice people argue it is every woman's right to decide what happens to her own body. And it is every child's right to be a wanted child.

The pro-choice position is that at least up to the point at which the fetus could live on its own outside the uterus, the fetus is tissue that a woman should have a right to remove.

Pro-choice people point out the potential harm for the mother and the child if the unwanted pregnancy were to continue. They would ask, for example, why pro-lifers would insist on punishing a 15-year-old pregnant girl by insisting she carry the child to full term. And they would point out that only half of the "children who have children" complete high school. So these child-mothers are more likely to depend on welfare.

Some pro-choice people would also argue that a child "destined" to be handicapped, or raised in a financially poor setting, or perhaps abused, should not have to face those problems.

Pro-life people, at the other end of the pendulum, are not convinced by the pro-choice argument that the fetus (Latin for *unborn child*) is merely tissue. Pro-life people say that factual and convincing evidence on the humanness of life in the uterus has come to light since 1973. Photographs and movies of life in the womb, surgeries performed on fetuses, and even abortions, have shown an active, responding, and growing human male or female person.

The major pro-life argument says that the fetus is a person, and has the right to be protected against harm, as does any other person.

Pro-life people remind us that in the vast majority of abortions, the mother chose to take the risk of getting pregnant, then refused to accept the responsibility for the consequences. And the pro-lifers ask why the fetus should be punished for the mistakes of the parents.

Some pro-lifers take this so far as to argue that the fetus should not be aborted for any reason, including rape, incest, or to protect the life of the mother. In the cases of rape and incest, they would argue that the fetus should not be punished for the sins of others. And in the case of being a threat to the life of the mother, they would insist there are two lives threatened, and only God should decide who will or will not live.

Methods of Abortion

The size of the unborn child determines the abortion method used. No method is easy, quiet, or comfortable. The developing fetus' body is usually torn and cut.

D & C. Abortion during the first three months of pregnancy is usually done by dilation and curettage (D & C). A doctor uses a surgical knife (curette) to cut the living fetus away from the wall of the uterus. Then the doctor inserts into the uterus a plastic tube the width of a large straw. This tube is attached to a suction machine that vacuums out the body parts and other contents of the uterus.

Most early abortions are done after the sixth week of pregnancy. The fetal heart has been beating rapidly for about four weeks. Physicians say that when they use amplification devices to listen to the heartbeat at this stage of development, it sounds like a roaring freight train. By this time, the unborn child has all his organs along with his own blood type. The unborn life is very active: swimming, doing somersaults, responding to light, sound, heat, and cold.

D & E. Dilation and evacuation (D & E) is done between 12 and 16 weeks. The doctor uses a sharp tool that looks like pliers. With this, the doctor grabs part of the fetal body and tears it from the uterine wall.

After the surgery, the abortion team often reassembles the body to make sure all parts were removed. Many abortions done in this the second trimester are because of fears the child will have genetic defects.

Intrauterine Injection. In most abortions after 16 weeks, the physician injects into the uterus, through the woman's abdomen, a saline (salt) solution. This salty liquid mixes with the protective amniotic fluid. The fetus swims in and breathes this corrosive solution. So the fetus is burned inside and out. On the outside, it can lose its outer layer of skin. Inside, the brine is absorbed into the lungs and digestive tract. Within 1 to 6 hours, the life is gone. This procedure usually induces a miscarriage within 12-24 hours. And the body is forced out by contractions, as with a normal delivery.

Surgery. In very late abortions, sometimes into the ninth month, doctors perform a hysterotomy (caesarean or

C-section). This removes the child through abdominal surgery. Sometimes abortions this late are done because the child will be born with a physical abnormality. But usually it is to protect the health of the woman. And usually, though not always, there are efforts made to keep the child alive.

Emotional Effects of Abortion

Listen to the testimony of a woman I know.[2]

"Have you ever been in an abortion clinic? I have. A few years ago a friend of mine found out that she was pregnant. Sally was 17 and could see no solution for her problem other than abortion. She was eight weeks pregnant. I went with her to the abortion clinic. She was taken into a room with 10 other girls. She was told what the procedure involved and that everything would be fine. This clinic did at least 100 abortions a day. ... Over the years Sally has said to me, 'I wonder what my baby would be doing today.' She blames all her problems on her abortion. Researchers are finding that post-abortion trauma is common and severe. Many women suffer from stress, have nightmares about the abortion, and deal with frequent thoughts of the aborted child. These problems can begin five to seven years after the abortion, or even later.

"As I think back on my experience with Sally, I feel badly. I wish I had known then what I know now. I could have helped her make the right decision."

In his book *Grand Illusions: The Legacy of Planned Parenthood* (1988), George Grant tells about how an abortion ended the relationship between Jared McCormick and his girlfriend Susie Glanze. Jared took Susie to Planned Parenthood for a pregnancy test.

"She was really scared, and so was I," Jared said. "I told her that we could go ahead and get married. We were planning on it anyway. We'd just have to move things up a little, is all. But she wanted me to finish up with school first. So, there we were."

The test was positive and Susie made an appointment at Planned Parenthood for an abortion the next Saturday. "I really went berserk," Jared said. "I was dead set against the abortion. I begged her to marry me and keep our baby. But she wouldn't listen."

The doctors performed a D & C. There was heavy bleeding, so Susie was rushed to the nearest hospital were she was given two units of blood and treated for cuts of the cervix and uterus. She remained in the hospital two days.

"It's amazing what can happen between two people in just a couple days' time," Jared said. "Susie was so grieved over what she'd done—over what they'd done—that she just couldn't stand to be with me anymore. Just like that. It was all over between us. I'm convinced that if she'd known how risky the operation was we'd be together today. And our baby would still be alive."

Education can be delayed. Jobs come and go. But the life aborted can never be brought back. This fact eventually torments a great many women who have abortions. The torment rolls in on waves of grief and shame. The emotional pain can lead to sexual promiscuity, eating disorders, anger toward those who did the abortion, separation from church and family, fear that others will find out about the abortion, and even suicide.

But there are women who are coming to grips with abortions they've had. Today women who have had abortions are speaking out more than ever before. Where are these women finding help in moving beyond their pain and secrecy? In churches and among pro-life groups.

Anne Speckhard, in her book *The Psyco-Social Aspects of Abortion* (1988), says that in this setting of support and concern, women who aborted can admit what they did and how they feel about it. They can talk about the abortion with people who will not deny the tragedy involved and who can understand the guilt abortion generates.

Where there is freedom from covering up, there is hope for healing. Many women who endured abortions are finding their way into a Christian community as they move beyond the secrecy and shame of the past.

My prayer is that their local churches will be ready to receive them.

---

1. Abortion laws are continually undergoing changes. Since *Roe vs. Wade,* the Supreme Court has given states more power to establish their own laws—a power states are beginning to exercise. This door was opened with the 1989 Missouri case of *Webster vs. Reproductive Health Services.* Here, the Supreme Court ruled that Missouri could (1) restrict the availability of publicly funded abortions and (2) require doctors to test for the viability of a fetus at 20 weeks, or two-thirds of the way through the second trimester.

2. From "You Are a Promise," visual production, copyright 1988, Families for Life. Used by permission. Sally is not the woman's real name.

Jean Purcell is a wife, mother, and founder of Families for Life, a lay ministry of the Church of the Nazarene since 1985. She and her husband are currently living in Geneva, Switzerland.

Chapter 6

Single Parents in Search of Help

by David Lambert

Background Scripture: Isaiah 1:10-17; 1 John 3:16-20

I'M WRITING this on Father's Day.

As a father of four kids between the ages of 4 and 13, I should have awakened to a fistful of dandelions in my face and black toast and massacred eggs on a tray.

Instead I woke to a dead house; the only sounds were

the ones I made rolling out of bed. A messy house, too—there hasn't been a lot of time for cleaning and straightening in the past couple of weeks as I've worked at my more-than-full-time job and tried to get the kids packed and ready for yesterday's train trip across five states to spend time with their mom.

They went. I stayed.

If it sounds like I'm feeling sorry for myself, let me explain: I'm glad for this little holiday from the kids, Father's Day or not. There were too many things I've been putting off because the arduous schedule of a single parent just didn't allow time.

Which brings up the first of many paradoxes single parents face: We're torn between our ferocious, protective love for our kids and our desperate, exhausted desire to be free of them for a while. It's a never-ending Catch-22.

Do you remember Joseph Heller's novel of World War II, *Catch-22*? The title refers to a military regulation that specified that a concern for one's own safety in the face of real and immediate dangers was the process of a rational mind.

A pilot could be excused from active duty if he were crazy. But if he tried to get out of flying his dangerous missions, then, according to Catch-22, he was sane—and had to fly them after all. A pilot "would be crazy to fly more missions and sane if he didn't, but if he was sane he had to fly them. If he flew them he was crazy and didn't have to; but if he didn't want to he was sane and had to."

Make sense? No? Then welcome to the world of the single parent, where every decision, every daily crisis, is regulated by Catch-22.

Day Care

Last year, with two preschoolers, I paid $105 a week for child care at a moderately priced, church-run preschool.

About $450 a month, $5,460 a year. I squeaked by because I had a decent job. But imagine the single mom I know with two preschoolers and one more in kindergarten. She'd be paying more than $7,000 a year in child care at that same preschool.

And what would her take-home pay be? One single mom whose husband walked out on her after 10 years of marriage, leaving her with four kids, was offered, despite her college degree, only one job—retail sales in a department store at $3.50 an hour, $7,280 a year before taxes. She can't afford to work, and she can't afford not to. Catch-22.

Trying to Be Two Parents

"Not too many years ago, American parents had a broad base of support in their task of child rearing," Andre Bustanoby writes in *Being a Single Parent.* "The extended family of grandparents, aunts, uncles, cousins, nieces, and nephews all had a part in rearing children and providing them with good role models. But with the growing mobility of the American population, the extended family began to shrink, and the task of child rearing became the exclusive task of the nuclear family—husband, wife, and siblings.

"Over the past 45 years, however, the nuclear family has taken a battering ... Child rearing—which was once the task of *many*—now is the task of *one.*"

Ironically, that task falls on the shoulders of the single parent at the worst possible time—when she is still grieving the loss of a spouse and a marriage.

"Being a single parent scared me half to death," Wendy says. "I didn't have any confidence whatsoever, either as a person or as a parent. I didn't know how I could manage two boys, raising them alone, trying to make decisions.

"I never thought I would want to beat my kids, but I was tired of having to be the only one to discipline them, wondering how I was going to manage. Eric had done something and

I just wanted to pick him up and throw him against the wall. I almost did.

"But all of a sudden something snapped, and I knew right then I had to get my act together, and I had to do it alone because there was no one else to help me do it."

The script varies a bit with the players: Single moms, especially if they have little boys, usually worry about discipline, and single dads usually worry that they're not being sufficiently gentle, understanding, and nurturing.

When I was married, I never realized how much I relied on my wife to fill in the gaps in my relationship with my kids: to be tough when I was sweet and sweet when I was tough. Now I have to be sweet with one hand and tough with the other.

It can be done, but try doing it day after day, week after week, crisis after crisis, tired or rested, in sickness and in health, and you'll understand why God made parents in pairs.

Finding a Place

One of the first hard realities a single parent stumbles across, after the shock of sudden singleness fades, is that he or she no longer has an appropriate place in society—even within the church.

"You don't feel comfortable with married, and you don't feel comfortable with singles," explains Lois. "Exactly where do you fit in? Finding a place is a difficult thing."

Even if you want to try the singles groups at church, most don't provide baby-sitting. And the singles without kids seem so like kids themselves. They're into dating. They talk about buying clothes, traveling, and shopping—activities the single parent doesn't have the time, money, or energy for.

"When we first separated," says Molly, a single mom of four, "I went to our singles group for a little while, and then

I quit going. So I tried the married Sunday School class again, but after a time I couldn't handle that either. So then I went to the Sunday School class for divorced people, but in that class I got so depressed I ended up crying every Sunday. I felt like I was in limbo, like I didn't fit in anywhere. I'm not 'single'—I've got these kids—but I'm not married either. I felt like I had no place."

The Quest for Normalcy

We just want to be normal again: to be able to handle our own affairs reasonably well, to be strong enough to be on the giving end once in a while instead of always needing something.

Instead, we struggle through our jobs, pick up the kids at day care, and rush all evening just to get the housework done, the bills paid, and the shelves stocked with food—and then realize as we're tucking the kids into bed that we forgot to make the doctor appointment and pick up the cleaning, and that we haven't said one constructive word to those kids all day. Too late. We stand and look at their sleeping faces for a few minutes, then fall exhausted into bed. Maybe tomorrow.

But tomorrow will be just like today. It has to be. As one single father said, "To have a career, to have a home that's well-kept, and to raise children the way you want to raise them cannot be done in 24-hour days. You either have to devote yourself to one or the other, or do them all less well than you could if you devoted yourself to one." Catch-22.

Real Help Wanted

Where is the church in all this? Single parents hear themselves talked about a lot in sermons these days. It's one of the "cutting edges" of Christian ministry. But for most single parents, that's just a tease.

"The pastor's been talking a lot about single-parent

families lately, about broken homes," Lois says. "I don't really see any change. It's one thing to preach about it; it's another thing to do something about it. I don't see any groups forming for single parents. I don't see the church extending itself toward us in any way—I don't see anything going on other than talking about it. People are aware of it—that's the only progress I see."

One single mom with no income other than her paycheck was laid off recently. Word spread quickly among the other employees, but most of them ignored her altogether, not knowing what to say. Their averted eyes hurt her immeasurably.

Others tried to stumble through some word of cheap encouragement, such as "Don't worry—you'll find another job soon. God has everything under control." But those glib, though well-intentioned, answers from people who had nothing to worry about only threw her deeper into depression.

One or two people, however, not knowing what to do, but unwilling to let her suffer alone, stopped to give her a silent hug and a compassionate, wordless look—and made it possible for her to endure that day and the days that followed.

In a sense, single parents are one more special-interest group in a list that includes starving children, victims of child or spouse abuse, the emotionally disturbed, the handicapped, the poor, and the aged.

What single parents are calling for is not merely stronger programs to meet their specific needs—although that is definitely needed. But beyond that, they are asking the church to grasp the clear teaching of Scripture that the vitality of our faith can be measured by the extent to which we "seek justice, encourage the oppressed. Defend the cause of the fatherless, plead the case of the widow" (Isaiah 1:17).

The apostle John states it this way: "If anyone has material possessions and sees his brother in need but has no pity on him, how can the love of God be in him? Dear children, let us not love with words or tongue but with actions and in truth. This then is how we know that we belong to the truth" (1 John 3:17-19). I hear an echo behind these words of John: "By this all men will know that you are my disciples," Jesus said, "if you love one another" (John 13:35).

"I can remember many times wishing," says Wendy, a single mom with two sons, "that someone would just say to me, 'We don't agree with what has happened, but we love you anyway and we're here for you, and if we can do anything, let us know.' But no one was saying that."

David Lambert is an editor with Zondervan Publishing House, Grand Rapids, Mich.

Chapter 7

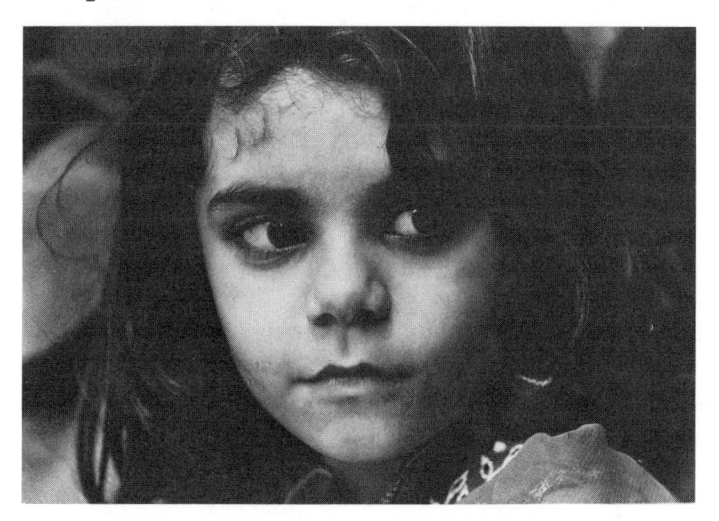

When We're Not Sure It's Child Abuse

by Scott Skiles

Background Scripture: Psalm 18:1-19; Matthew 5:43-44; Galatians 6:2

CHILD ABUSE: grown-ups hurting children, sometimes killing them.

I don't think there's another issue that so stirs our emotions and sparks such an immediate and universal cry of condemnation. For almost everyone, there is absolute clarity. No need for discussion. No reason for debate. No shades of gray. Child abuse is absolute evil.

Tragic cases like those of Eli Creekmore and Lisa Steinberg, children who died at the hands of a parent and whose cries for protection went unheeded, solidify our strong convictions. These are cases that rally people together. With our hindsight, the need for action seemed obvious: The children should have been taken out of their families. Even the trauma of being taken from their homes would have been better than the deaths that occurred when they stayed.

Borderline Cases Around Us

For most of us, though, the child abuse we see does not usually involve this level of brutality. And neither are we sure about the need for action.

Instead, when we see hints of abuse and cases of borderline mistreatment—on the job, at home, in our church—our clear-eyed fervor melts into uncertainty.

How many of us have stood by and watched a neighbor, friend, relative, or church member treat their child in a way that made us uncomfortable?

Perhaps we felt the words were a little too cruel.

Or the spanking a little too hard.

Or the children a little too young to be left alone so long.

Or the adult a little too affectionate.

Or the child a little too knowledgeable about sexual matters.

These are the kinds of tensions we are more likely to face. No observable marks or scars. No clear-cut disclosures. Just a nagging discomfort that leaves us feeling unsettled.

We think "someone" ought to do "something," but what? Should someone talk to the parent? Should someone notify police or protective services? What if we're wrong?

What about the damage this could do to the relationship between the parent and us, or between the parent and child? These are only a few of the questions we grapple with when we find ourselves tripping over what might be clues of child abuse.

Daddy's Girl

Even when we're sure a child is being abused, there can be great uncertainty about what to do. Recently a pastor called me for advice on how to handle a sexual abuse situation in his church.

The 12-year-old daughter of a respected leader in the church had confided to an adult woman friend that her father had started fondling her at bedtime. The daughter insisted that her friend not tell anyone. But the friend felt she had to at least tell the pastor. When the friend told him, she said she would leave the matter with him. She would not confront the father or notify the authorities. The pastor had to decide what to do.

Consider just a few of the questions he faced.

If he confronted the father, would the daughter feel her confidence had been betrayed and would she refuse to confide again in her friend?

Would the daughter's friend feel betrayed by him?

What would happen if he confronted the father, and the daughter denied the allegation—which is common among young victims?

Should he report this to the authorities and risk alienating the entire family? (Pastors, by the way, are not legally required to report such suspicions.)

How might this hurt the daughter if she found herself in a foster home?

What about how this news would shatter the mother, whom the daughter said had no idea what was happening?

There are no easy answers.

These questions and more confront many pastors, teachers, relatives, and friends of children who are being abused. Before we consider possible solutions to the problem, let's make sure we understand exactly what abuse is.

Four Kinds of Abuse

Each state enforces a host of abuse laws. Though there are some differences from state to state, almost all states divide child abuse into three categories: physical abuse, neglect, and sexual abuse. Some add a fourth: emotional abuse.

1. Physical abuse. This involves a person who physically and on purpose hurts a child. To describe physical abuse, lawyers use phrases like "willful cruelty" and "unjustifiable punishment." In California, where I live, it can involve corporal punishment—spanking—that leaves marks after several minutes.

2. Neglect. This happens when a person responsible for a child's care neglects the child in a way that can harm the child's health and welfare. The term includes both acts and omissions on the part of the responsible person.

Examples of neglect would include not providing food, clothing, or medical attention; leaving a child unattended; placing a child in a potentially dangerous setting.

3. Sexual abuse. This includes two categories: sexual assault and sexual exploitation.

Sexual assault includes rape, incest, sodomy, and what the law describes as "lewd and lascivious behavior," which can include a broad range of sexual actions.

Sexual exploitation involves child pornography.

4. Emotional abuse. Many states also have laws that attempt to address the issue of emotional abuse. This involves intense verbal abuse and the type of cruelty that tries to break the child's spirit rather than the body.

Though this abuse is perhaps the most common, protective services workers and district attorneys will also tell you it is one of the hardest to prove and prosecute.

First Course of Action: Prayer

Because of the potential consequences of our actions on behalf of children we think are being abused, we need wisdom beyond human understanding.

No amount of training, education, or experience can take the place of bringing these children and their problems before the Father. Our first course of action should be to prayerfully seek the wisdom and compassion of God.

However, even when we have sought His direction, sometimes our uncertainty remains. One reason for this hesitation is because we realize no matter what we do, someone could get hurt. There is no way around that.

If a child is being mistreated and we choose not to intervene, the child will suffer pain ranging from a crushed spirit to a broken body. And if we confront the parent or notify authorities, the parent could face the possibility of broken relationships, of having to leave home, or even of imprisonment. There are also times when well-meaning interveners place the child in what should be safe surroundings, only to have the child suffer more abuse and pain from temporary guardians.

Last year in the United States, over 2 million cases of abuse were reported, according to the American Humane Society. Over 20,000 of these involved major physical abuse.

In addition, some experts conservatively estimate that one in four girls in the U.S. will have at least one unwanted sexual contact with an adult before age 18.

These are difficult, intense, and complicated issues. But after several years of dealing with children and families suffering from abuse, I am absolutely convinced that those of us who cling to the hope of Christ are also called to advocate on behalf of the vulnerable and the victimized.

There is no comfortable way to get involved. Don't bother looking for it—it doesn't exist. Involvement brings discomfort, uneasiness, and conflict. So when we ask for God's wisdom, we do well to ask also for His courage.

What We Can Do

Though every situation is unique and calls for an individual approach, we can identify three general courses of action.

1. Confront the parent. This can be difficult and uncomfortable because the parent or caretaker usually responds with hostility and defensiveness.

The closer our relationship is with the parent, the better chance we have of being heard. Also, the more we identify with the parent's stress, pain, or feelings of inadequacy, the more effective our discussion can be. Once abusive parents get over the initial defensiveness, many will talk about how unhappy they are with the way they are treating their child. Providing emotional support—sometimes even tangible support, like a hand on the shoulder—can go a long way in helping an overwhelmed parent and in creating a safer environment for the child.

2. Notify the authorities. These are usually city, county, or state child protection agencies.

When we notify authorities of a potentially dangerous situation, that does not mean the child will automatically be taken from the home. Often, protective services workers try to help families while the child remains in the home.

A report to protective services can be anonymous and does not have to be accompanied by overwhelming evidence. When we make a report, we are simply asking the protective services worker to evaluate the situation to see if indeed there is mistreatment.

As in any organization, there are some protective services workers who are more competent and committed than others. Notifying authorities can usually be productive, helpful, and essential to the child's safety. But sometimes it can also be a frustrating, disillusioning, and counterproductive endeavor. Because of this, I recommend to pastors and teachers that they get to know at least one protective services worker in their community. When the workers know you and trust you, they are more likely to take you seriously and provide effective help for the child and family.

3. Confront the parent AND notify the authorities. The dynamics of sexual abuse are too intense to be handled only informally. Authorities should always be notified if a child is at risk for sexual abuse.

If we are to help a vulnerable, victimized child, we need to hold the abuser accountable both spiritually and legally. If we simply keep the matter informal, many sexually abusing parents or family members will admit to the abuse and give heart-felt pleas for a second chance and genuine "guarantees" never to engage in the behavior again. (In most cases they do this only after the child's disclosure.)

But this isn't enough. The abusers need more than a second chance. They need professional help.

This "hard line" approach is the abuser's best hope for getting the help and healing he needs.

Let's take the example we talked about earlier of the pastor who was trying to help the young girl who said her dad had been fondling her.

The pastor struggled and prayed over what to do. He and I talked several times. He concluded that he had to put the girl's safety and well-being above all else. So he convinced the daughter's adult friend, who had first learned of the abuse, to meet with him and the daughter.

During that meeting, the daughter admitted her father had been fondling her. Twice, he had tried to have intercourse with her. The daughter also said she was worried the father may have started fondling her eight-year-old sister. The daughter and her friend later talked with the eight-year-old, who denied any abuse.

The pastor then met with the daughter, the friend, and

the mother. He told the mother what the daughter had disclosed. The mother was understandably devastated and initially said she was not sure if she believed her daughter, since the girl had been recently "acting differently" and getting in trouble at school. The pastor said he believed the daughter, as did the daughter's friend.

Next, the pastor met with the father alone and confronted him with the allegations. The father became angry and denied the abuse. At that point, the pastor told the father that to protect the daughter, he was going to have to report this. The father then threatened to sue the pastor.

After the pastor reported the abuse, the court temporarily placed both daughters with an aunt. The children remained with the aunt through the court proceedings. The 12-year-old girl suffered through the emotionally traumatic and humiliating experience of testifying in court.

In the end, the father was found guilty, and agreed to a long-term therapy program as an alternative to jail. The mother and father separated and the children were returned to their mother, who still expresses some doubt about whether or not abuse took place.

Though the mother no longer attends the church, she still allows her children to go. Both girls are involved in the church and receive encouragement from the pastor and congregation.

If you think this true story does not have a completely satisfying resolution, you're right. And welcome to the uncertainties of dealing with child abuse. Someone always gets hurt. This family paid a heavy toll for the abuse and its remedy. Some of the relationships may never heal completely. And even yet the family faces a difficult road ahead.

But something good happened, too. A couple of young girls were protected. Life-changing abuse was stopped. And a message was clearly sent to the victim that even though she was experiencing great pain and trauma, she was not alone.

I believe this girl's pastor and friend embodied the love and courage of Christ. They stood beside her in her pain and became her advocates. They got involved. They became uncomfortable, upset, and full of conflict. They did the best they knew how and took action in the real world, where situations are rarely clear-cut and easily resolved.

This is what we are called to do, also.

And as we get involved—as we advocate, struggle, encourage, confront, and love—we need to remember that we, too, are not alone. The advocating, struggling, encouraging, confronting, loving Christ is with us.

Scott Skiles is a licensed, clinical social worker at Children's Hospital, Oakland, Calif. He formerly directed a child abuse intervention program in Los Angeles.

Chapter 8

What Kind of Man Would Beat His Wife?

by Kay Marshall Strom

Background Scripture: Ephesians 5:22-33

As SOON AS JANET SAW ROGER at the door, she knew what was coming. Fortunately the children had already had their dinner, so she hurriedly sent them upstairs to watch television and then get themselves to bed.

"Be careful," Janet told herself. "Everything has to be just right. Stay calm and don't do anything to upset him."

Roger growled about having had a terrible day at work. Janet nodded sympathetically, but she was careful not to speak. Past experience warned her that anything she said might be the wrong thing.

Glancing around the living room, Roger spotted a stack of magazines Janet had intended to take out to the trash. "This place is a pigpen! Don't you ever clean up? What do you do around the house all day anyway?"

Janet mumbled an apology and rushed over to get rid of the magazines.

"I'm starved!" Roger growled. "What's for dinner?"

Janet caught her breath. This is it, she thought. He's not going to like dinner, and I'm going to get it.

"I asked you, what's for dinner?"

Panic welled up inside her. Struggling to keep her voice even and controlled, she answered, "I made meatloaf and mashed potatoes—lots of mashed potatoes. I know how much you like them. And there's apple pie for dessert. It will be on the table in a minute."

To her great relief, Roger said nothing. Maybe she had been wrong. Maybe this wasn't going to be one of those nights. Maybe, just maybe, things were going to be different this time. And so she let down her guard.

When Roger saw the dinner table, his eyes flashed and his jaw stiffened. "Why did you have to use the tablecloth your mother made? You know I don't like it!" He grabbed the tablecloth and jerked it off the table, sending plates, utensils, glasses, and platters of food crashing to the floor.

Terror seized Janet. This is it, she thought frantically. I've got to get out of the house. I've got to get away.

But the children were upstairs; she couldn't just leave them. Unsure of what to do, she hesitated. And then it was too late.

Grabbing her by her hair, Roger threw her to the floor. He hit her again and again. He called her horrible names. He tried to choke her. Janet begged him to stop, but her pleas only made him angrier. The last thing she remembered was her head slamming against the floor.

When Janet woke up, she was lying on the sofa. Roger was standing over her. "I'm sorry, Honey," he said. "I'm sorry I had to do it. Why do you have to make me so angry? Why can't you do things the way I ask you to? If you would just obey, I wouldn't have to punish you like this."

Janet and Roger first met in college. Although he was four years older than she, they were in the same class. "He is so mature!" she had bubbled over the telephone to her sister, Lenore. "He was in the navy for four years, so he's much older than the other boys around here. And he is so interesting! He's been everywhere and he's done everything. Not only is he handsome, he's smart, too, and a good athlete, and thoughtful and considerate."

"Nothing like Dad," Lenore had commented dryly.

As a matter of fact, Roger *was* the opposite of Janet's father. Perhaps that's what made him so attractive to her. While her father was loud and boisterous and bossy, Roger was quiet and sincere and considerate. Janet's family had never been religious—especially her father, who insisted that any man who couldn't run his own life didn't deserve to be called a man. It was different in Roger's family. They called themselves Christians and were all active in their church. Patiently, and with feeling, Roger had told Janet about his own personal relationship with Jesus Christ.

"Christian men are good and kind and loving," Janet told Lenore. "Christian men aren't like our father."

"He sounds like the catch of a lifetime," Lenore said with a laugh. "I think you should marry that man!"

And that is exactly what Janet did. Actually, she would have preferred to wait until they graduated, but Roger was insistent. He was ready to settle down. "Besides," he pointed out, "you don't need a college education. One wage-earner in the family is enough. I want my wife to stay home with the children where she belongs."

The first year of married life was wonderful. Janet persuaded Roger to let her work at the switchboard in the administration building of the college while he finished school. She enjoyed her job and loved being a part of college life. And she was so proud of her new husband! Not only did he get academic honors, but athletic awards were heaped on him as well.

Not that their marriage was perfect. But then, what marriage is? For instance, it soon became evident that Roger had a much quicker temper than Janet had expected. At times she was at a loss to understand what she had done to set him off. When he was angry he said cruel, insulting things to her. One time, when she tried to defend herself from his insults, he slapped her face. After that she kept her mouth shut and tried to remember that he talked that way only because he was angry. He didn't really mean it.

Then came the day Janet went off to work and unintentionally left the front door of their apartment unlocked. Taking advantage of the open door, someone came in and robbed them of their new color television set, a camera, and a radio. Janet was upset and angry with herself, but Roger was livid. He screamed and yelled at her and called her "stupid," "fool," and "idiot."

"If you're going to act like a child, I'll have to treat you like a child!" he yelled. "You will have to be punished!"

Roger's punishment loosened two of Janet's teeth and blackened her eyes. She was horrified at his violence. But, she reasoned, she had deserved it.

"I'm sorry," she told Roger through her tears. "From now on I'll be more careful, I promise."

Janet thought this would be the end of the problem, but she was wrong. It was just the beginning.

Common Myths About Wife Batterers

Roger is a confusing combination of violence and gentleness, cruelty and love. What is it that causes a seemingly normal, caring husband to turn into a batterer? What kind of men are batterers?

Everyone has inadequacies. All husbands, like their wives, sometimes lose their tempers. But not every husband grabs his wife by the hair, pulls her to the ground, and kicks her in the face.

The problem of wife abuse is complicated by the myths surrounding the issue. When a man does not fit the stereotype of a wife abuser, people find it hard to believe that the battering is really going on. How could such a nice guy be capable of beating his wife? What Janet's friends don't understand is that there is no such thing as "the abusive type." This denial by friends and associates only reinforces the batterer's belief that his actions are right in the eyes of God and man. Consequently, he sees no reason to change.

Here are some of the most common myths about wife beaters, followed by the facts. You may be surprised.

Myth 1: *Wife battering is a problem of lower-class families.*

Fact: Batterers are found in all levels of society and cut across all economic, racial, ethnic, religious, and geographic lines. They can be doctors or lawyers or college professors. They can be mechanics or plumbers or politicians. They can be rich or poor, educated or illiterate. Every segment of our society is affected.

Myth 2: *Batterers are losers—financially, socially, and emotionally.*

Fact: Like Roger, many wife beaters are successful, churchgoing, well-liked, nice guys. They are often charming and pleasant to others; many are highly respected in their communities. People outside their home frequently see them as good providers, warm and loving fathers, caring husbands, and law-abiding citizens. Only their families see the violent side of these abusive men.

Myth 3: *Wife beaters are sick, psychotic men.*

Fact: Certainly some are, but counselors tell us that by far the majority lead normal lives in every way except that they are unable to control their aggression. Although many batterers do seem to have two personalities, unlike true psychopaths they usually feel a deep sense of guilt—and shame—for what they have done.

Myth 4: *Because they have usually been drinking, battering men can't control their violent behavior.*

Fact: Drunkenness, like mental illness, is one of society's conventional explanations of wife beating. While it is true that many batterers were drinking just before an attack, many experts maintain that abusive men use their drunken condition as a convenient excuse for their violent behavior. Alcohol may be the trigger that lets loose a man's pent-up rage and violence. Then again it may merely be a cover-up for violence that was going to happen anyway. "I didn't know what I was doing—I was drunk" is an often-used and often-accepted excuse.

Myth 5: *Wife abuse does not affect Christian families. Christian men do not act this way.*

Fact: Wife abuse does occur in Christian homes. One need only look at the recent rash of articles on the subject, and the stories they relate, to prove this. After a special section on wife battering appeared in a Christian family life magazine, the editor stated, "The relevance of this topic to our readership was emphasized by the record number of letters sent to us from Christian women who are or have been victims of wife abuse . . . more than we have ever received in response to any article in the magazine."

Characteristics Common to Batterers

While there is no such thing as a typical abuser, there are characteristics that are common to many abusive men.

The majority were raised in abusive homes. Over half of all abusive men were either themselves abused as children or else witnessed their fathers abusing their mothers. Less than one-quarter had what could be called good relationships with their parents.[1] Domestic violence has a nasty way of reproducing itself generation after generation.

Most are unable to communicate effectively. Battering husbands tend to find it very hard to understand and express emotions other than anger. Anxiety, fear, frustration, affection—all of these end up being expressed the same way. Their physical violence is not usually an expression of anger toward their partners, but rather more likely a ventilation of their own feelings of inadequacy and frustration. Many experts feel the violence of wife beaters is the result of pent-up frustration and anger that has been repressed.

Most batterers believe in sex-role stereotypes. Many are overly concerned with living up to a tough, self-sufficient, masculine role. They believe a husband should be in charge, his every word unquestioned law. Many were raised to regard women as childlike or as possessions. They believe their position as man of the house gives them the right to direct and control their wives and, when necessary, to punish them and to force compliance.

Over and over police hear the same astonished, indignant response from abusive husbands: "You mean I can't beat my own wife?"

The majority have a deep need to hide their weaknesses and insecurities. Many, many batterers suffer from crippling insecurity, immaturity, and self-doubt. By being physically dominating, they try to reassure themselves that they really are strong and in control. Because they feel weak and powerless, they resort to violence as a way to prove their power and masculinity.

Although they go to extremes to present a "macho" image, batterers are highly dependent on their wives. That's why a batterer is particularly dangerous when his wife threatens or tries to leave home. Beating her is his one chance to be the oppressor instead of the oppressed. Through physical force these men seem to gain the sense of power they are unable to feel anywhere but at home. It is not hard to understand why husbands who are unemployed or dissatisfied with their jobs are more likely than others to abuse their wives.[2] Because they lack a sense of control over their own lives, they determine to at least control their wives.

Batterers often fear losing their wives. Because he so desperately fears losing his wife, the batterer often tries to make her stay close to him by being possessive and jealous. He may even attempt to isolate her from her friends and family. Afraid that she will become friendly with someone, he may refuse to allow her to get a job. He may go so far as to check her car mileage and time her errands. If she's late, or if her mileage doesn't check out, he is convinced she is seeing another man—so he beats her.

Because free access to money gives a woman some degree of freedom, many abusers maintain complete control over the family's finances. When other methods of exerting control fail, they may resort to threats, either to kill their wives or to kill themselves. And these are not always empty threats.

Their wives are a convenient scapegoat. The wife beater has no idea who he is really trying to hurt. Although it's small comfort to his injured wife, she likely is not the one he really wants to destroy. The real target may be his parents, or perhaps his business associates, or even himself. So why does he strike out at his wife? Because she is the most accessible target and she has little chance of escaping or getting back at him. Furthermore, he knows that society is not likely to interfere.

They often blame their abusive behavior on their wives. It is next to impossible to get an abusive man to admit he has a problem. Like Roger, they often blame their wives for their violent outbursts, even though the woman may have done nothing more than choose the wrong tablecloth.

For most there are times of remorse. It's not unusual for the batterer, when he sees the truth of what he has done, to become frightened and to try to make up to his wife. But even while apologizing and pleading for forgiveness, few batterers can accept the responsibility for what has happened.

There are men who, although they fit many of these characteristics, never show any signs of violence toward their wives. There are also successful husbands who don't drink, were raised in healthy families, show signs of good self-esteem, and demonstrate no jealousy, who nevertheless beat up on their wives. *It is important to understand that the characteristics mentioned here only put a man at risk of becoming a batterer.* But being at risk is not the same as being destined to act in a specific manner. Whatever contributing factors and tendencies exist, in the end the responsibility falls upon each person to decide his own actions.

What Can Be Done?

Is there anything we can do? Absolutely! All it takes is a few concerned Christians who see the need and are ready to get involved.

Any group can provide practical assistance to victims of abuse. When emotionally distraught mothers need to have their children out of the house for a time, volunteer babysitters can give them the break they need. Women who flee their homes need help in locating housing and finding jobs. Many need financial assistance. All need nonjudgmental support, encouragement, and prayer.

Judi Bumstead, director of Family Ministries at Trinity Baptist Church in Santa Barbara, Calif., is one who would like to see the Christian community take action. A licensed marriage, family, and child counselor, Judi has had the opportunity to work with battered women, and she has specific suggestions for local Christian groups who want to help by counseling these women.

As a first step, Judi suggests forming a corps of individuals who really want to make a difference. They need not be professionals, but they do need to be trained. It is dangerous and unfair to ask even the most well-meaning volunteers to work beyond their training and experience.

For groups without access to such professional Christian organizations, Judi Bumstead suggests looking to a resource that is available almost everywhere—the community shelter for battered women. Because they are generally underfunded and understaffed, most shelters welcome volunteers. In exchange for their services, volunteers will be trained and will have an opportunity to gain experience that could be helpful to the Christian community.

When a violent man is out of control, the thing his wife needs most is a place of safety for herself and her children. Churches have traditionally been known as places of sanctuary. It can still be so.

Without a doubt there is a real need for more shelters, especially ones that operate from a Christian point of view. The problem is that setting up and maintaining a shelter is a difficult and expensive task, one that few churches have the personnel or the finances to undertake.

Judi Bumstead suggests creating a network of homes from different churches in the community, so that women will be able to be sheltered in places their husbands would be unlikely to look.

When talking about the support group she attended at a community shelter, June, a minister's wife, said, "In my support group I said exactly what I felt and no one hated me for it. I told the others what my husband had done to me, and never once did they tell me it was my fault. I was accepted and understood. Those women knew from firsthand experience what I needed, and they were ready and able to give it to me."

After several minutes June added, "But I also had questions they couldn't answer—questions about submission to my husband, about God and why He let this happen to me. I would really have appreciated a Christian perspective. Why don't churches sponsor groups like that?"

To establish a support group, all that is needed is a place to meet, a trained leader, and a couple of people willing to be involved in the group. A small beginning is fine. Word will get around. Notify the local Salvation Army chapter, the community women's shelter, Christian counselors, the YMCA and YWCA, and local churches. Make it known that there is a Christian support group available for abused women.

An Ounce of Prevention

The best way to deal with family violence is to help prevent it from occurring in the first place. The church's preventive role is, in the long run, the most important of all. By developing an in-depth program of premarital counseling—one that realistically approaches subjects such as anger, conflict, and violence—a couple can discuss what each will do should violence ever occur. They should be encouraged to set ground rules with each other in advance and to establish a fair and workable way of dealing with the conflicts that are sure to arise in their marriage.

But family education should not stop with premarital counseling. Parenting classes, marriage enrichment workshops, family communication workshops—all of these are excellent opportunities to help families learn how to shape and develop relationships in nonviolent, supportive, positive ways. By equipping families to develop caring, nurturing, loving relationships, the cycle of violence can be broken.

Epilogue

After another attack, in which Roger nearly drowned Janet by holding her head under water in the bathtub, Janet went to her bedroom and took the suitcase off the top shelf of the closet. She packed a few necessities, a change of clothes, the cash she had carefully hidden away, the checkbook, several documents, and the children's baby pictures. Then she took down another suitcase and packed several outfits for each of the children.

From her beside table she picked up her new Bible with the burgundy leather cover. Opening the front pages she read this inscription: "To my dearest Janet, whom I will love forever. Your husband, Roger." As she tucked the Bible into the suitcase, her eyes filled with her first tears of the evening. "Oh, Roger," she whispered, "why does it have to end like this?"

Janet tiptoed into her son's room and gently shook the sleeping child. "Get up quickly, David, and don't make a sound."

"What's happening, Mom?" he asked, rubbing his sleepy eyes.

"Never mind. Just do as I say. I'll explain it later."

"Is it Daddy?"

"I'll explain later," Janet said again. "Put on your jacket and shoes, go quietly out the back door and wait in the car. I'll get Christy, and we'll meet you there."

Janet and her children went to Marilyn's where they were welcomed and made comfortable. After tucking the exhausted little ones into bed, Marilyn made a pot of hot tea. Then she sat and listened as Janet poured out her story of anger and frustration. Marilyn hugged her when the tears came, and asked her no questions.

"Did I do the right thing?" Janet asked. "Was I right to leave him?"

"Your life was in danger," Marilyn replied. "You did what you had to do." Reaching over, she took Janet's hand.

Janet and her children stayed with Marilyn for almost a week, long enough for her to make some serious decisions. She determined that no longer would she subject herself or her children to Roger's uncontrollable rage. She would not go back to him without evidence of repentance. Together they would make a written agreement of the rules of their home—in particular her right to be safe from violence, and commitment from him that he was ready and willing to change his behavior. He would have to prove that commitment by getting treatment from a qualified counselor, and he must stay with it long enough for her to see that he was committed to it—six months, she decided.

At the end of the week Janet moved into an apartment nearby. Accompanied by Marilyn and her husband, Janet returned to her house to collect her and the children's belongings. Though Roger knew they were coming, he chose not to be home.

Janet had always believed that marriage is for keeps. Even though Roger's brutality had splintered their vows to love, honor, respect, and cherish, she didn't want to call it quits. As far as she was concerned, this apartment was just someplace where she could be safe while Roger realized his action and attitudes were sin and completely out of line with biblical guidelines. She wanted them to get back together, but she had come to realize that unless Roger realized he had been wrong and unless he sought to change, he would continue to abuse her.

A long, rough road lies ahead for Janet. The years of abuse cannot be erased overnight, nor even in weeks or months or years. No one should expect that. Whatever happens, scars will remain.

Yet the end to Janet's story is one of hope, one of promise. And why not? God is real. He is all-powerful. He is faithful. And He holds those who suffer close to his heart.

---

1. "Black and Blue Marriages," *Human Behavior Magazine* (June 1976).

2. One of the first to touch on this subject: John E. O'Brien, "Violence in Divorce-Prone Families," *Journal of Marriage and Family* (November 1971, vol. 33, No. 4).

Kay Marshall Strom is the author of several books including *Helping Women in Crises* and *Chosen Families* (Zondervan). This chapter was adapted from the book *In the Name of Submission,* by Kay Marshall Strom, copyright 1986 by Kay Marshall Strom. Published by Multnomah Press, Portland, OR 97266. Used by permission.

Chapter 9

Children in Thailand

Simple Living: From Barbecued Rat to $700 Million for Chewing Gum

by Larry Dinkins

Background Scripture: Matthew 6:19-21; Luke 18:18-29; Philippians 4:10-19

MY WIFE AND I were exhausted, having recently returned from Thailand where we had spent four tough years as church-planting missionaries. We were ready for a vacation. My mother offered to send us to a 2,300-acre Christian resort for a week, and having heard of its first-class, 500-room hotel and its reputation as the Christian Disneyland, we jumped at the chance.

After we passed through the park gates, we walked into the lobby of the grand hotel, unprepared for the cultural shock. We had been used to mud, dust, and flies. Now we were standing in an ornate lobby with a harp and a Steinway grand piano. The contrast between the wealth and luxury surrounding us and the poverty and hunger of Thailand was too great.

My wife and I had been born with the proverbial silver spoon in our mouths, growing up with all the advantages of upper middle-class suburbia. We knew convenience, cleanliness, privacy, and rapid transportation.

But in Thailand, such "necessities" were rare. So we decided to simplify our lives, and we discovered that we could still live well with plain foods, public transportation, simple clothing, and humble housing. But simplifying our life-style was more than just a practical decision, it was biblical.

Products of Muchness

Our mission asked us to live at the level of a Thai teacher, so when we arrived in Thailand, we moved into a small shophouse in a fresh-food market. During our stay in the market we observed that some of the very poor in our area were eating barbecued rats caught in the local rice fields.

Eating rat would repulse most Americans, who spend more than $700 million a year on chewing gum and seven times that much on pet food. But 60 percent of the world lives on *less* than 2,200 calories a day, the minimum necessary to maintain good health. They welcome the protein from rat meat.

America is a nation of wealth. Most people have the money and resources to eat whatever they choose. Yet more than 1 million of them a year suffer heart attacks.

"Maybe heart disease is God's way of telling us we're living too high on the hog," said one sick executive. "It's hard to practice moderation in this country. We're a nation of excess." Or as Mother Teresa said, "The West is suffocating from muchness."

As products of that excess and muchness, my wife and I had difficulty adjusting to living at the level of a Thai teacher. The church we worked with consisted of the illiterate and poverty-stricken, with a smattering of lepers. We felt we were making serious sacrifices to live as they did. But to them, we were fabulously wealthy. Our plane fare alone was many times the yearly wage of the average Thai.

"Do you know what they're paying for rent?" asked Uncle Chan, introducing us to the church. "Fifty dollars a month. Can you believe that?" He could afford only $15.00 We had many lessons to learn about living simply.

We had arrived in Thailand with two large barrels and several trunks of "necessities." Within two months, our home was robbed five times and most of our prized luxuries were taken.

It was just as well. Most of what was taken was really unnecessary, and even hindered the Thais from accepting us. We started to understand Matthew 6:19-20: "Do not store up for yourselves treasures on earth, where moth and rust destroy, and *where thieves break in and steal.* But store up for yourselves treasures in heaven" (italics added).

Still, we felt anger and loss. Like a parent trying to pry a toy from a selfish two-year-old, God had to loosen our grip on our material things. Simplifying our life-style was hard, but God showed us there are two biblical reasons to do it: to help the poor and to help finance evangelism.

Helping the Poor

Thailand's economy is controlled by a rich minority, while the masses remain poor. It has been a common scenario since biblical times, which is why the Old Testament prophets were constantly demanding a just distribution of wealth.

Modern-day prophets are still speaking out. "How can we be indifferent," Billy Graham said several years ago now, "to the millions and millions who live on the brink of starvation each year while the nations of the world spend $550 billion each year on weapons?"

Jesus said, "You will always have the poor among you." But He didn't mean that the "haves" can neglect the "have nots." I grew up isolated from the poor in our community, always carefully avoiding the other side of the tracks.

In Thailand we couldn't avoid them. Beggars passed by our door daily, cup in hand. Sometimes I scrambled for my 35-mm camera to get a candid shot before they passed. Then it struck me. My camera equipment alone cost almost as much as a Thai's annual wage, and I finally sent it back home and bought a simple pocket camera.

Jesus taught, "From everyone who has been given much, much will be demanded" (Luke 12:48). The United States, with only 5 percent of the world's population, possesses 54 percent of all wealth and 80 percent of all wealth among Christians. Surely God requires much of us in helping the poor.

Financing Evangelism

God requires much in respect to people's souls, too. Around the world, more than 2.4 billion people have never heard a clear presentation of the gospel—almost 50 million of them in Thailand. Only 60,000 Thais are considered Protestant Christians. And in central Thailand, where we lived, only one in 4,000 was a Christian. Many people I spoke to knew more about Santa Claus than they did about Jesus.

The West has exported its technology, music, and expertise to the Third World, but had failed to supply its people's spiritual needs with the gospel. Christian literature, television and radio programs, and thousands of churches inundate the West. Many hear the gospel hundreds of items, while in other parts of the world, people have never heard. That's why I left the comforts of my home to work as a missionary in Thailand, why I simplified my life-style.

Christians are commanded to evangelize the world. But to raise the funds required for the task, many Christians will need to simplify their life-styles so they can contribute more.

One way to do this is for Christians to commit themselves to living on the same salary as missionaries on furlough. By living more simply, basing their spending decisions on the needs of the poor and for evangelization, they can help finance more missionaries.

Biblical Life-styles

The Bible doesn't say at what economic level Christians should live, but it does provide principles that can help determine what pleases God.

The Ten Commandments speak of life-style. The first two commandments prohibit idolatry, and with more than 26,000 temples and spirit houses, Thailand is full of idols. Yet the West is full of idols, too.

Americans don't burn incense to new boats or fall prostrate before VCRs, but their bondage is real. Biblically, anything that takes God's place in our lives is an idol. Materialism, with its emphasis on acquiring more money and things irrespective of need, leads to idolatrous life-styles. Idolatry can have no place in a Christian's life.

The 10th Commandment condemns covetousness, or

the desire to keep up with the Joneses. Paul called it greed and equated it with idolatry. "Put to death ... greed, which is idolatry" (Colossians 3:5; see Ephesians 5:5).

But God doesn't condemn wealth. After all, Job, Abraham, and Solomon were wealthy men. What He condemns is its misuse. To Israel's rich He said, "I will not turn back my wrath. They sell the righteous for silver, and the needy for a pair of sandals. They trample on the heads of the poor as upon the dust of the ground and deny justice to the oppressed" (Amos 2:6-7).

Jesus taught that there are inherent spiritual dangers in riches. Yes, He said that life is to be enjoyed. But He also said that it is foolish to hoard and evil to covet (Luke 12:13-21), that riches tend to blind us to the needs of the poor (Luke 16), and that wealth is a barrier to total commitment to God (Luke 18). Riches don't damn, but they make salvation more difficult. The implication is that it's right to give away one's surplus.

But in His clearest teaching, Jesus said, "Sell your possessions and give to the poor. . . . For where your treasure is, there your heart will be also" (Luke 12:33-34).

Contentment and Living Simply

Paul often wrote about conformity to the world, moderation, giving, and greed. But the core of his teaching about Christian life-style is Philippians 4:11: "I have learned to be content whatever the circumstances." And being content without luxuries was something he had to learn.

It's a difficult lesson. Pastor Chuck Swindoll said, "It is hard to be content when we've been programmed from birth to compete. . . . We're afraid of contentment because if we accept it we're either lazy or will lose prestige."

The symbol of how I've learned contentment is my old-fashioned shaving brush. In Thailand, shaving cream costs more than $5.00. I couldn't afford that much, but the Noxema girl had convinced me that if it was not medicated, heated, or scented, it wouldn't work. Searching for an alternative, I discovered that shaving cream is merely soap. Over the next four years, I saved more than $60.00.

Madison Avenue's goal is to breed discontent. Christians must not follow ads, but find contentment in a secure relationship with Jesus Christ.

In Thailand, I knew a leper whom people called Mr. Itch because he was always scratching his skin. Despite his illness, he was fairly well off, owning his land debt-free and able to save a little money with his wife's help. But his shirts could be counted on one hand, he owned a $5.00 watch that he couldn't set, had no transportation, a fourth-grade education, no electricity, and no modern conveniences.

Yet Mr. Itch was content—more so than many Christians in affluent America—deeply rooted in his relationship with Christ.

Paul said he was content *whatever the circumstances.* There is no one right biblical life-style to which all Christians must conform themselves. There are no rules to follow in buying that new sofa or car. The Bible doesn't tell me whether I should buy a new house or remodel the one I have, or whether to use a conventional stove or a microwave.

But God has provided principles to help us determine what our life-styles should be. In a word, Christian life-style is a matter of attitude. What is our attitude toward material things? Do we use riches or do they use us? Is money our servant or are we its slave? All wealth belongs to God. We are merely temporary stewards of that bounty.

Four years in Thailand caused our family to evaluate our attitudes and life-style. And as we prepared for a second term on the mission field, we actually looked forward to the simpler Asian way of life. No more clock watching or television, no more ringing telephones or cancer-causing diet drinks.

Yet God doesn't expect all Christians to adopt the life-style of missionaries, only to live more simply. Perhaps more Christians should consider this resolution of the Lausanne Committee for World Evangelization: "All of us are shocked by the poverty of millions and disturbed by the injustices that cause it. Those of us who live in affluent circumstances accept our duty to develop a simple life-style in order to contribute more generously to both relief and evangelism."

Larry Dinkens is a missionary working in Thailand with Overseas Missionary Fellowship.

Chapter 10

How Churches Can Fight Drug Abuse

by Jerry Hull

Background Scripture: Romans 14:13-21; 1 Corinthians 3:16-17

SHE LIVED in my hometown. But I never met her. I only read about her and talked with people who knew her.

She was a faithful little league mother. She invested hours in driving, waiting, and cheering. Coaches and teachers knew her well. No one had been more persistent in keeping her children involved in athletics. She figured it was a small price to keep them away from alcohol and other drugs.

Her efforts were rewarded. Her oldest son made the starting line-up on the local high school football team. Then later, during the winter of his senior year, he took home the big trophy as state champion wrestler in the heavyweight class.

Mother and son enjoyed their shared achievements. Together they planned for his college years. A plush college scholarship was going to allow the young man to reach new levels of athletic competition.

Mom's work was not done, though. Her younger children were also involved in school athletics. Plenty more hours of driving, waiting, and cheering awaited her when the next school year began.

Alcohol slaughtered this dream of partnership between a mother and her children.

It happened in the dusk of early evening. She passed through the green traffic light at 12th Avenue and Greenhurst Road. Just a few yards beyond the intersection an oncoming car swerved into her lane. It wasn't far to Mercy Hospital, less than a mile. But by then she had become another DOA statistic, dead on arrival.

An investigation confirmed that the driver of the errant car was drunk.

This drinking driver had fulfilled one of alcohol's commitments to Americans. Every year, year after year, alcohol vows to kill 25,000 Americans in automobile wrecks.* Twenty-five thousand sounds like a lot of people, yet it is just an impersonal number—until the tally includes a person we know.

I wonder how many times the champion wrestler cried like a lost little boy as he grieved for his mother? How many sleepless hours did he stare into the darkness of his dormitory room, remembering his mom jumping up and down on the sidelines, cheering him on?

We hate the suffering and the waste that alcohol and other drugs create. We love to hate drugs. Politicians, especially those running for reelection, stumble over each other sponsoring antidrug legislation. Hundreds of organizations promote education aimed at halting drug abuse.

What's going on? Why have all the antidrug strategies failed?

Hating drugs is commendable, but it's not enough. In spite of our concentrated hate and all of our strategies and manpower, drug abuse seems to be winning in the war on drugs.

But the war isn't lost—if we can learn more about drug abuse, develop wiser strategies, and enlist more people in the conflict.

Why Get Involved?

Why should we spend our time, energy, and money opposing drugs? After all,

- No one close to me is a user.
- Everyone has hang-ups. Is drug abuse really any worse in God's eyes than overeating, or lying, or speeding?
- All our efforts won't make a dime's bit of difference. Drug abusers will always be with us.

Concerning this third excuse, there's a story about a youngster who was walking along the coastline, where thousands of starfish had washed ashore. As the young fellow walked along, every now and again he would pick up a starfish and heave it back into the safety of the ocean. An old man saw this and asked the youngster, "Why are you doing that. There are miles of beach. What difference could you make by throwing back a few starfish?"

The boy picked up another, threw it in the water and replied, "Made a difference to that one."

Why get involved? How about the following reasons—just a few of the problems caused by drug abuse: crime, injury, illness, birth defects, death, loss of productivity, family arguments, and separation.

What Drugs Are We Talking About?

Drugs that can be abused include any chemical substance that alters our physical or mental state. These include:
1. Prescriptions used differently than doctors instructed
2. Household and industrial products used as inhalants
3. Mind- and body-altering chemical substances defined by law as illegal
4. Alcohol and tobacco

Let's take a quick look at some of the drugs now creating havoc in our society. We need the facts to help us put up a decent fight.

Alcohol. This is America's most popular drug of choice. It is promoted by more than $2 billion a year. The alcohol industry uses these billions in advertising and in sponsorships of everything from beauty pageants to races. Because of this kind of exposure, is it any wonder many claim alcohol is the "gateway" drug—the first drug people try?

In our society, it is normal to use alcohol. That makes those of us who don't use it abnormal. In fact, 7 out of 10 adults—count 'em—use alcohol. Nine out of 10 college-age young people at least occasionally drink it.

Almost 7 out of 10 teenagers admit to drinking it once in a while. Eight out of 10 consume alcohol in the year before their high school graduation. An even more frightening fact is that in one recent survey, 4 out of 10 teen drinkers admitted to binge drinking in the two weeks before the survey. "Binge drinking" is considered five or more drinks in one sitting.

Let's admit it. We have a serious national problem, especially among our young people. We realize this when we remember that the purchase and use of alcohol before age 21 is illegal in all 50 states. But should we be surprised at the widespread use when we learn that 100,000 of the million TV commercials a youngster sees before age 18 are for alcoholic beverages? That's 1 out of every 10 commercials. Add to this all the advertisements youngsters see on billboards, in magazines, in newspapers, and in sponsorship of sports and community activities. The message we send our young people is clear. Alcohol belongs.

Given all these cultural and advertisement pressures, it is gratifying that 30 percent of adults choose not to drink. Those of us committed to abstinence need to take courage. Our nonalcoholic stance is valuable and defensible.

The first 1 to 3 drinks (regardless of body weight) slow brain functions. It is absorbed into the bloodstream, mostly through the small intestine. It provides an initial "high," followed by a feeling of relaxation, loss of inhibitions, dulling of attention, weakening of self-control, a false sense of confidence, and impairment of judgment. Long-term abuse can lead to brain disorders, cirrhosis, and birth defects.

Tobacco. The tobacco leaf has proven to be a sturdy foe. We hope to oust it from society, but it is putting up quite a battle. In 1963 the United States surgeon general announced that the U.S. was going to war with tobacco.

For more than 25 years, warnings have accompanied all cigar and cigarette advertisements. And more recently they have been added to ads on chewing tobacco. In addition, warnings appear on packages containing the products. Research stacked on research affirms the conclusion with consistent monotony: It is dangerous to use tobacco in any form.

Yet, after more than 25 years of antismoking campaigns, nearly 30 percent of our adults still smoke. The percentage of users declines slightly each year. This is commendable.

Each day, however, 1,000 Americans die as a result of tobacco use. That's 350,000 preventable deaths—enough people to fill four Super Bowl stadiums.

That's a high price to pay to maintain income for tobacco farmers and others employed by the industry.

With all this dying going on, it seems insignificant to talk about nonsmokers who have to breathe the stuff second-hand. A few years ago, while I was spending a few hours in Sun Valley, Idaho, I saw an interesting T-shirt. Inscribed on it was this message: "If you won't smoke I won't vomit." There have been times I've wished I was wearing a shirt like that.

Marijuana. Recent research reveals that nearly 60 percent of high school seniors have experimented with marijuana. About 25 percent of high school students smoke marijuana at least occasionally.

Some symptoms of marijuana use are lowered inhibitions, relaxation, talkativeness, loss of concentration, mood swings, and increased pulse rate. Continued use may result in paranoia, delusions, and hallucinations.

Steve Miller, the editor of this book, tells me he knows of an alcoholic man in his early 30s who had beaten alcoholism but thought he could handle marijuana.

"During the man's month of rehabilitation in the hospital," Miller said, "he started smoking marijuana again. When his counselor confronted him about it, the young man admitted what he was doing and assured the counselor he could handle it.

"The counselor said that not only could the alcoholic not handle marijuana, there was a host of over-the-counter drugs he absolutely had to stay away from."

Well, the young man insisted he could handle the weed and that he would keep on smoking it. The counselor responded by saying the young man would then be booted out of the rehabilitation program, and would have to pay the hospital bill himself. (Insurance would not pay unless he completed the program.) So with this financial motivation, the young man swore off marijuana. Eventually, he became convinced he could not handle the drug. Today, he does volunteer work with other alcoholics and drug abusers.

Inhalants. These are almost as popular as alcohol, tobacco, and marijuana. Inhalants present special problems because they are so easy to get. They present a daily temptation to young children. Dozens of products are available to sniff. Household glue, gasoline additives, lighter fluid, typewriter correction fluid, paint thinner, paint, varnish, fingernail polish, polish remover.

Vapors from these products act as depressants on the central nervous system. They impair vision, reduce muscle control, slur speech, and create exhilaration from lightheadedness. Overuse may result in damage to the brain, liver, and nerves. In extreme cases, inhalants can lead to a coma or death.

I read of a man who beat drugs and eventually landed a construction job in the organization of a well-known televangelist. But the man was recently fired because coworkers caught him sniffing a can of paint in the nearby woods. He had "fallen off the wagon" with the help of an inhalant that was all too available to him.

Steroids. The current emphasis on a beautiful body and athletic strength make today's youth unusually vulnerable for steroid use. Perhaps half a million young people are using steroids. This synthetic derivative of hormones is used to increase muscle mass and strength.

But the gains of the drug are offset by the risks, especially to young people who are still developing physically. Risks include greater likelihood of ligament and tendon injuries, mood changes, acne, stomach pain, hives, loss of appetite, blurred vision, and nosebleeds. Continued use can lead to heart disease, liver damage, sterility, and impotence.

Cocaine. This substance is possibly the most potent of all the brain stimulants. It comes from the leaves of the

South American coca plant. When sold on the streets it is diluted with any number of a wide variety of substances. So it often ranges from 5 to 80 percent purity.

News commentator Paul Harvey offered a solution to users who were complaining that dealers were cutting their cocaine with the rat poison D-Con. Harvey said police have a test to determine the presence of foreign substances in the drug and that they would be happy to perform the test for anyone who brought in their cocaine.

Cocaine (or a cheap and highly addictive variant known as crack) is, unfortunately, used by up to 9 percent of teens. Perhaps a total of 6 million Americans use cocaine. It stimulates the pleasure nerves in the brain. There is a rush of euphoria, energy, confidence, and talkativeness. It can also increase the heartbeat, breathing rate, generate depression. Overdoses can bring on convulsions, stroke, respiratory failure, heart attack, coma, and death.

Cocaine is a growing problem for newborns. A recent survey of 36 hospitals across the country found that of 155,000 births, 17,050—11 percent—had been exposed to illegal drugs. The most commonly used drug was cocaine.

Dr. Howard Kilbride described his first encounter with a cocaine-addicted baby at Truman Medical Center in Kansas City. "The baby ... had a seizure shortly after birth. At the time, I contacted some toxicologists to try to figure out what was going on. I thought it was withdrawal, but they indicated it was a direct toxic effect." The doctor said he later learned the mother had sniffed cocaine to ease the discomfort of labor pains before coming to the hospital. "The baby," he said, "had overdosed on the mom's cocaine."

What Should the Church Do?

1. We should clearly state the strong arguments against drug use. Two of the strongest Christian principles in fighting the war on drugs are: *(a)* We are God's temples, and *(b)*

We are to avoid doing anything that will negatively influence others.

Paul makes the first principle clear. We are the temple of the living God (see 1 Corinthians 3:16-17; 6:19-20; 2 Corinthians 6:6; 7:1). We are not to abuse His dwelling with improper care.

We also find in the New Testament some powerful verses that instruct us to control our behavior so we do not influence negatively a weaker brother (see Matthew 18:6; Romans 12:10; 14:1, 13, 21; 1 Corinthians 8:9).

2. We should know the facts about drug use.

3. We should show compassion and support to victims of drug abuse—both the abuser and the family of the abuser. It is easy to avoid the parents who have a prodigal son or daughter on the "far country" trip of drug use. The family needs tender, loving care and affirmation. The drug abusing son or daughter needs prayer, attention, and love.

4. We need to form alliances with other churches and organizations in the community that are committed to battling drug abuse. And we need to invest time and money in our shared causes, and take a more active role in the fight.

5. We should give attention to two specific issues within the church. We need to teach our children how to say no to drugs. And we should instill in them the healthy self-concept they need to resist the pressure their schoolmates will put on them to "just try it."

We might not be able to do all of these things—at least not at first. But we can at least get started by doing one of these things. Whatever we do could make a big difference to someone. Just remember the beached starfish.

---

*Alcohol is involved in four times this number (100,000) of deaths each year if we include all accidents and crimes linked to alcohol.

Jerry Hull is professor of social work at Northwest Nazarene College, Nampa, Idaho.

Chapter 11

What Churches Are Doing (or Could Be Doing) for the Disabled

by Dorothy I. Baird

Background Scripture: Romans 12:1-13; 1 Corinthians 13

SEVERAL YEARS AGO I wrote a book about our 36-year-old daughter Dorothee, born with cerebral palsy. Actually, she started the book 10 years earlier. With a dowel wand fastened to her headband she laboriously typed, "Mother, help me write my story."

When I got the invitation to contribute to this book you are now reading, Dorothee again inspired me to accept this new challenge. She gave me messages of encouragement each time my husband and I visited her home near us.

On a December day recently, one of her therapists called. "Mrs. Baird, Dorothee is inviting several of us to a Christmas party at your home. Is that OK with you?"

"Of course," I tried not to act too surprised. "Just let her know how many and a convenient night. I'm delighted to host her party."

Happiness filled our home the night of our party. Dorothee's strategy worked. I was drawn more deeply into her circle of God's beautiful people. We looked at slides of a trip the group had taken to California in October. Ten aides and therapists had accompanied Dorothee and six others in wheelchairs on a plane trip. They were attending an international conference on speech communication. They also visited Disneyland. We laughed at pictures of completely inadequate, ridiculous ramps and rides marked "wheelchair accessible."

After we chatted a while, I asked the therapists if some of them would tell me why they chose to work with handicapped people?

Kathy, a therapist, who raised thousands of dollars needed for the California trip, said, "The clients' friendship draws me. They give me so much more than I give them. I'm working with people who care."

Kathy, you're so gracious and intelligent, I thought. You could command a top executive position. Yet you choose to work as a servant.

Then Valerie, a shy redhead in her early 20s, and one of Dorothee's aides, spoke. "Before I started at the Residence

Center, I had a good job in retail. But I hated to waste my life serving people who lived only for material things." Valerie was being transferred to another wing. Dorothee would miss her. They had become good friends.

Valerie carpooled that night with Bill, a rough looking character with a black beard and shaggy long hair. He spoke with compassion. "I earned over 30 thou before. But who needs that much money? I'm really happy now, doing some good."

Sheila explained, "Until I became a Christian a year ago, I never really loved anyone. But now I love the disabled and I am accepting their love." Sheila had accompanied Dorothee to a Bible conference at an ocean beach camp.

Most Churches Are Doing Nothing

After Dorothee's party, I better understood why the apostle Paul proclaimed that love is the greatest gift of all. But the party also left me confused. It was love that had drawn the therapists to the handicapped. But what has caused the gap between the church and the disabled? It is a rare church that ministers to the disabled. Only about 5 percent of American churches have programs for them.*

Many church leaders say they have no such ministry because there are no disabled people in their church. Perhaps they should ask why these people aren't there. One of every 10 people in a community, on the average, is disabled. There are more than 32 million in America, according the National Center for Health Statistics. That's about equal to the population of New York state and Texas combined. These people suffer from disabilities such as crippling arthritis, blindness, deafness, Down's syndrome, epilepsy, and paralysis from spinal cord injuries.

Yet the vast majority of these people are non-Christians. Common estimates are that between 85 and 95 percent of disabled people are not associated with any church.

What Churches Can Do

How can churches begin ministering to disabled people in their communities, and at the same time find a fulfillment like that of the therapists at Dorothee's party? My husband and I recently took a 10,000-mile trip, visiting churches across the country, to find out.

Based on what we saw, here are some ideas I think most churches—large and small—can consider.

1. Have a handicap awareness Sunday. This introduces the need to your congregation. For one such service I helped with, in a Presbyterian church, we installed ramps and removed some of the church pews. We got help from disabled Christians in the community, and asked them to take charge of the service.

A group of mentally and physically disabled people ushered. A blind man used his braille Bible to read scripture. Dorothee wrote the prayer of confession, which was read by a friend in a wheelchair and was signed by a deaf woman.

A man with a rare blood disease offered the main prayer. He thanked God for Christians in the congregation who had donated blood to keep him alive. "But," he added, "the greatest gift of all is the blood of Your Son, shed for me so that I, by accepting it, will live forever." A few months later, the man died. The sanctuary was packed for his memorial service.

Instead of preaching a sermon the day of the handicap awareness Sunday, the pastor interviewed a man who had been paralyzed from the neck down in a car accident.

The pastor also commissioned a young woman who was going to serve the church as a missionary to Lisbon, Portugal. She would become a traveling teacher who would train mentally handicapped children and their parents. In less than three years, this woman has started a school and has written a series of lessons missionaries use with the mentally disabled.

As part of the day's events, we held a hands-on fair in nearby classrooms. Each guest watched demonstrations of mechanical devices used by the handicapped, and were invited to hold these devices. We displayed books, tapes, and slides. Then we enjoyed a picnic in which the disabled and the abled became acquainted in a friendly, happy atmosphere.

This was a pretty elaborate program. As you can imagine, it took a lot of planning. But handicap awareness services don't have to be this elaborate. Free packets on how to conduct a smaller-scale service are available from some church headquarters and from organizations such as Joni and Friends, Inc. Joni's packet includes a suggested order of service, detailed sermon outline, news release for the local paper, taped message from Joni, congregational survey, and a church access checklist.

2. Conduct a church access audit. We owe it to disabled people to provide them a way of taking part in worship and Sunday School.

My church is in the process of remodeling. The Sunday it was announced that our new building would include elevators to every floor, Dorothee squealed her sound of joy. It was her way of saying, "Amen!" The congregation clapped their approval.

3. Provide transportation. At the very least, identify the most convenient parking spaces as "Handicapped Parking." One church I know of has a trust fund to pay for taxi service.

4. Use the talents of the people in your church. In my church, people our taking seriously Romans 12, and making themselves living sacrifices.

Lee, a beautician, cuts hair without charge.

Diane, an artist, led an art class for the disabled.

Barbara, a retired teacher, tutors an autistic child.

Ainar, an executive, drives the disabled to special events, like concerts.

Agnes, a seamstress, sewed over 100 bibs.

Young athletes drive the disabled to sports events. Dorothee seldom misses a home football game.

5. Make room for wheelchairs. Adults who are confined to wheelchairs should feel welcome in worship services, Sunday School classes, and all church events.

Some churches take out one or more pews, to make room for people in wheelchairs. Others shorten some of the pews, so the people in wheelchairs can blend into the crowd without sitting in the front, the back, or the aisle.

6. Budget for the disabled. Programs for ministry to disabled people should become part of the church budget.

7. Begin a weeknight program for the mentally disabled. Colonial Presbyterian Church in Kansas City says this is more popular than Sunday School. About 15 to 20 attend the 1-hour Sunday School. But 45 to 50 attend the 2½-hour Monday night program. One reason the Monday program is more popular is partly because it allows students—ages 2 to 50—to do more. They rotate between four stations: Bible study, games, prayer, and crafts. This also allows a night out for the caregivers, who can drop off their disabled loved one, then have a couple hours to themselves.

8. Provide free time once a week to those who take care of disabled family members. This is called respite care. Everyone needs a break from the routine, especially those who have the 24-hour-a-day task of taking care of disabled loved ones. Perhaps the respite care could be nothing more than a weekly 1- or 2-hour visit in the home, while the caregivers go out for a meal or for shopping.

9. Survey your congregation. Ask them for names and addresses of disabled people in their neighborhood. Contact these people and ask how they think the church could help people like themselves.

After you discover what kind of disabilities people in your area have, you are in a better position to know where to begin your ministry. It is best to focus on one kind of disability before branching out into ministering to other disability needs.

10. Call the disabled. Even if it's just to wish the person a good day, to read them a verse from the Bible, or to say a prayer. For some, especially for those we often call shut-ins, this can be a highlight of their day.

The Haunting Words of a Blind Woman

Sometimes I wonder who is more disabled, the handicapped people, or the churches that fail to minister to them.

I'll never forget the words of a blind woman. At a handicap awareness service, she asked:

Who Is a Handicapped Person?
The one who can't see;
or the one who doesn't look?
The one who can't hear;
or the one who won't listen?
The one who reaches out with only one hand;
or the one who is afraid to reach out at all?

---

*From a survey conducted by John Wern of Joni and Friends, Inc., P.O. Box 3333, Agoura Hills, CA 91301. This survey included only the half-dozen or so denominations with a full-time staff person assigned to disability concerns. Wern said he believes the percentage would be lower in denominations without such a staff person. At this point, none of the denominations in the holiness movement have such a full-time staff person. The Church of the Nazarene has a part-time staff member assigned to disability concerns.

Dorothy Baird works with disabled people in her local church and is author of *Dorothee: The Silent Teacher*, a book about her daughter who was born with cerebral palsy. She lectures and serves on local and national committees for disability concerns and has taught special education. She lives with her husband in Seattle.

Chapter 12

The Graying of the Church

by Tim Stafford

Background Scripture: Exodus 20:12; Job 12:12; Isaiah 46:3-4

I RECENTLY ATTENDED a conference at which Christian "senior leaders" discussed what would be their legacy to a younger generation. White-haired gentlemen greeted each other with backslaps; they had known one another for a long time, or at least had read each other's books.

Many of these men still led sizable institutions. Yet they

did not act like a small club trying to hold on to dwindling power. They spoke keenly of the demands of our times, and seemed anxious that a younger generation be empowered to tackle them. "Whether we like to admit it or not," several said, "our day is coming to a close."

Such magnanimity often characterizes the elderly. In my own church, seniors are among the fiercest in insisting that we have an outstanding youth program. As they put it, "The young are the future of the church."

While admiring this generosity, I believe it has become dangerous—an old virtue out of place in these new times. For it assumes that the world belongs to the young, and that the elderly may (and should) retire into the background.

Yet America increasingly belongs to the old. Those white-haired leaders, ready to retire into the pleasures of travel and golf, are far from finished. In 1933, when the new Social Security Administration set the age of retirement at 65, most 65-year-olds were within a handful of years of death. Now, 65 is quite young. The average American, retiring at 63, has between 15 and 20 years of good health ahead. If seniors opt out of the challenges of the coming century, if they retire into senior hedonism and toss away a quarter of their adult life, we will lose our wisest, most experienced leaders before their time.

And if the church neglects the elderly, overlooking their needs and their potential because we are so used to focusing on young families, we will miss a key opportunity. In a rapidly increasing sense, the old are our future.

Toward 20 Percent Senior Adults

Today about 11 percent of Americans are over 65. That proportion will gradually rise over the next 15 years, and take a big jump when the baby boomers start turning 65, in 2010. Meanwhile, Americans have not been reproducing at a rate that would replace themselves. Ultimately, the proportion of seniors should peak between 18 and 22 percent—about double what it is today.

Many churches are already there. James Ellor, professor of human services at Chicago's National College of Education, has found that in any given American community, church attendance will include about 10 percent more elderly than the community at large; thus, if a certain town has the national average of 11 percent over 65, its churches will be about 21 percent elderly.

The mainline denominations particularly confront aging membership. About one-quarter of Presbyterians, Episcopalians, and Methodists are over 65, and about half are over 50. These denominations are consequently doing the most to organize ministry with the elderly. A Methodist seminary, Saint Paul's in Kansas City, has the nation's first endowed chair of gerontology at a seminary. The professor, David Oliver, says some of his students will have ministry experiences in rural churches where 100 percent of the congregation is over 65. There are some churches in the Sun Belt, ministering to retirement communities, that are also overwhelmingly made up of the elderly.

A Pair of Crises

The aging of America will pose national crises of two kinds. The most obvious is financial. The twin miracles of Social Security and Medicare, combined with the huge tax breaks for pension plans, have made older citizens better off than the population at large. A significant minority remain tragically poor, without even the theoretical possibility of working their way out of poverty. But 20 years ago the elderly were poor as a group. Now they are, by some measures, the wealthiest sector of America. The difference is almost entirely due to government spending. Let no one say you cannot solve poverty by throwing money at it. We did.

This huge cash transfer was almost painless because it coincided with the coming of age of the baby boom. A rapidly expanding labor force made it possible to spread the increasing cost over a growing pool of workers. Now, however, the field has begun to reverse itself. When the baby boomers hit 65, something will have to give. It is projected that payroll taxes for Social Security would reach 25 to 30 percent just to maintain the current level of benefits. This could provoke a major crisis—perhaps even a conflict between the generations.

But another subtler crisis could come: a crisis of national self-image. Americans have seen themselves as idealists—the "city on the hill" image—and as pragmatists—the "can-do" image. It would be difficult, given our current way of thinking, to associate either image with a nation dominated by retirees.

We have seen how the baby boomers skewed the thinking of the nation toward each generation they were passing through: toward family life when they were children in the 50s toward idealistic protest when college students in the late 60s, toward economics and entrepreneurialism when young workers in the 80s. Toward what will this lean when they are retired? Golf? It is hard to imagine, today, that an old America will find it easy to think proudly of itself, or to feel purposeful. We will need a better interpretation of what it means to be old.

The church should lead in this reinterpretation. But right now it is part of the problem. Carol Pierskalla, who heads senior programs at American Baptist headquarters, complains, "I hear pastors say, 'What can I do with this church? I look out and see that all the heads are gray.' It's that kind of ageism that will do us in."

Fortunately for us, that kind of ageism is not found in Scripture, not in one single verse. We have a source of guidance to help us change our thinking.

The Church's Response

How should the church respond to the aging of America?

Aging in modern America has two distinct characteristics. First, for the majority, it is leisure: premature and long years of leisure by the standards of all earlier eras. (Seniors may be very busy, but they usually have considerable choice in how they spend their time.) Then, for at least a large minority, aging is distinctively loss, usually gradual and cumulative over as much as a decade. And unlike Horatio Alger, unlike Scarlett O'Hara in *Gone with the Wind,* unlike refugees from war-torn Germany, these losers will never make a new start.

As aging is both leisure and loss, so the church's response must be in two kinds. First, older Christians must make something purposeful of this long stretch of life called retirement. Second, older Christians must find meaning and spiritual growth through the losses that often accompany their last years on Earth. These responses are essential if we are to reclaim the biblical idea of old age as a blessing (Exodus 20:12; Job 12:12).

While many church programs begin by concentrating on ministry to the dependent elderly—the homebound or those in convalescent hospitals—there is increasing recognition that most of those over 65 are hale and hearty.

Church ministries specially designed for the "young old" typically involve Sunday School classes, a midweek luncheon or Bible study, educational trips, and retreats. These programs may appear to be like entertainment-oriented youth programs; but they fill an especially important role in the life of seniors. Aging people often find their circle of human contact limited by the fact that they no longer work, that they are less able or motivated to get out, and that their circle of friends has begun to die off. Social contact is a vital need.

But few people involved in seniors ministry are content to provide only social programs. Says David Oliver of Saint Paul's Seminary, "When I first came here everybody was talking about ministry to the aging. Now it's shifted to ministry *with*. I'm thinking maybe we need ministry *from*. They probably can teach us more about our faith than anybody. Who else has been in relationship with God longer?" Adds Pat Parker, who ministers to older adults at Pennsylvania's Drexel Hill Baptist Church, "It's the retired in our churches who have the time to give to the community. I get really upset with pastors who say, 'Oh, my congregation is all grayheaded.' That's where your money is, that's where your energy is. Young people have energy, but we don't have it to give to the church."

The most common way of using retired people in the church is to involve them with ministry to those still older than they—to visiting the homebound, for instance. Presbyterians have launched the "Gift of a Lifetime," a kind of VISTA program in which retired people volunteer two years to go to another church and develop ministry to the elderly. "Part of the issue is a call to older people, 'What does the Lord require of you?'" says Thomas Robb of the Presbyterian Church (U.S.A.) Office on Aging. Adds psychologist Coleen Zabriskie, "I don't see any permission in Scripture for us to retire from serving the Lord."

Yet it is often the old who disqualify themselves. "There are two barriers I've seen from the start," says David Jobe, pastor for senior adult ministries at First Evangelical Free Church in Fullerton, Calif. "One is, 'I won't get involved because I've done my part.' The other is, 'I can't. I couldn't do that, I'm too old for that.'"

"Often older people pull back in retirement and rest," notes Janine Tartaglia, of Pasadena's First Church of the Nazarene. "That's OK. There's a place for rest. We need to retreat. But we need to remember that we shouldn't go into retreat forever." She recommends that churches help people plan in advance what they want to accomplish during retirement.

Many pastors to the elderly also encourage retirees to plan for their own death or disablement. Not only is there great practical value in thinking through funerals, wills, and the degree of medical intervention they wish in the event of a serious disease. The planning process may also deepen spiritual growth, as the older Christian confronts the losses that will occur.

The "Old Old"—All but Forgotten

If the "young old" should be challenged with their potential for service, the "old old" (those over 85) challenge the younger church to serve them. When people become homebound, or even unable to talk intelligibly, do they remain members of Christ's body? In many churches they are all but forgotten.

Serving the homebound means opening avenues for them to continue a life of service, through prayer, through the telephone, through the mail, through routine tasks that can be done at home. One of the worst parts of being homebound is a sense of uselessness and isolation. James Ellor says, "When people are no longer able to participate in worship there is a period of withdrawal, of real unhappiness." He notes that many find a "functional equivalent" in the electronic church, and suggests church leaders should recognize and even offer counsel about this through a list of preferred TV programs.

Pat Parker emphasizes the church's responsibility to stay in touch. "I hear them saying, 'I gave my life to the church. Was it worth it? Now when I expect some return, where is it?'" Janet Yancey, who runs an inner-city seniors program at Chicago's LaSalle Street Church, notes, "There's no bang for the bucks when you're working with older people. Some would say the best you can expect is that they're going to die. Young people have great potential. They're going to be missionaries. They'll earn money and pour it into our program. Old people are going to get crabbier and sicker. But God's command to me is not to put my money where there is a big bang. His command is to visit the homeless and the widowed."

Programs involving the "old old" tend to meet very practical needs. Many churches sponsor convalescent home visitation and worship services, and give home Communion. Some churches attempt to keep in touch with members through volunteer visiting or telephoning teams, who can touch base on at least a weekly basis. Often tapes of Sunday services are hand-carried to elderly members, and at least one church has used taped "calls to worship" from homebound members to begin Sunday worship. James Ellor cites a church that organizes one-on-one Bible studies in the homes of the homebound.

Other churches work to provide "Meals on Wheels," transportation, or escort services. Says Yancey, who uses 25 church volunteers in a Homebound Elderly Program, "They need someone to take them to the bank. They're not steady on their feet, they're nervous, they're not used to being out there. They don't want someone to do it for them. They want help—for balancing their checkbook, grocery shopping, going to the doctor, paying bills. We must build programs to meet their needs. They may not need another Bible class."

Our Challenge

Our challenge is to understand old age as something good. That means treasuring and caring for those whose ability to contribute or attend church is diminished. That means considering a congregation that has grown predominantly old as full of opportunity and hope. That means seeing seniors as people with great potential for ministering to others.

It may also mean, especially in rural or urban areas, reconfiguring our image of evangelism and church growth. James Ellor describes a church on the west side of Chicago that has a nursery filled with practically antique toys. "Everything is in its place, which is a bad thing to say about a nursery. It means nobody is using it." The congregation, he says, has come to see that nursery as a symbol of what is hopelessly wrong with it: There are no young people to fill it with children. "If you ask the elderly how to make a church grow, they'll say bring in the young." But there are very few young people left in the neighborhood.

Ellor is not so sure the old members are right. "Maybe they need to have a sale and get rid of those antique toys. Maybe they should use the proceeds to put in a senior center. What is wrong with reaching out to widows?" In the decades ahead, more and more churches will need to ask that kind of question.

Tim Stafford is a senior writer for *Christianity Today*. This article is copyrighted 1987 by *Christianity Today* and is used by permission.

Chapter 13

Building Bridges to Your Neighbors

by Tom Eisenman

Background Scripture: Luke 10:25-37; Romans 13:9-10

WE CHOSE our neighborhood carefully. We bought our home on a cul-de-sac made up predominantly of young families. It was important for us to have that traditional family feel: married couples with young children starting their lives together. We wanted community, shared lives, a network of caring.

The first thing we noticed when we moved in, however, was that people did not seem as eager to meet us as we were to meet them.

Our moving day was ignored. Later we found out why. Every few months another neighbor would move, so why make a big thing of it?

We had chosen a middle income neighborhood that was a good place to buy into, build some equity, and move up. People were cool toward us, but it made sense. Why spend time getting to know a family if they were just going to move out a year later?

We tried to be friendly. We prayed for our neighbors and asked God to give us just one good relationship to build on. But for the first few years, it didn't happen. Instead, we watched the neighborhood collapse.

In a little over three years we lost several traditional families. We found ourselves living on a block with three divorced women trying to make a go of it with their children, a young couple dedicated to a life with two careers and no children, a male homosexual couple, a house full of college students, and a family with five teenage boys—each with his own pickup. They lived in the two bedroom ranch across the street.

We started thinking about moving ourselves. Our children were growing, and we were cramped for space. It was either move or add on. We prayed about this for some time. Finally we decided to build an addition and stay. Judie and I couldn't help thinking that God may have placed us in this neighborhood for a reason.

As the new room went up on top of the garage, the neighborhood took notice. The addition was a symbol of something new for our block. A family was choosing to sink their roots down deeper.

It had a tremendous impact. Many in the neighborhood suddenly seemed to trust us more. Choosing to stay and build was a visible statement of our commitment to them and to the neighborhood.

After nearly four years, we began to see some things opening up. The modern couple next door came to dinner. Afterward they told us they had never had so much fun with children before. They began inviting our kids to their home and into their yard to jump on the trampoline. Within a year, she was pregnant, and they made it clear that it was being around our kids that helped them decide to expand their family.

After their daughter was born, the woman went back to work, and Judie sat with the little girl during the day. This was the beginning of a fine friendship. After we invited them to a Christmas concert at church, the woman started coming to church regularly. She is still struggling with how Jesus Christ relates to her life, but we're certain that something good will come from her honest questioning.

Then a woman down the block who lives alone with her son became very ill. Even though we had talked only a few times, she was open to our help. She especially wanted to know more about the church and its programs for kids. Recently she went through the new members class, and her teenager is enjoying the junior high program.

Breaking Down Barriers

Even if you live in a more stable neighborhood, it is still becoming harder to relate to your neighbors. When you knock on someone's door you don't know what to expect. You can't be positive that the couple living there is married, or if this is their first marriage. Neighborhoods have become a mix of nationalities, cultures, and life-styles.

Most neighborhoods have little communication. People choose to live in isolation. This is where we come in. Christians have a reason to reach out in love.

We have our model in Jesus, who attacked all barriers to relationships, whether class, cultural, or national. He spent time with religious leaders in the community, and He ate with prostitutes and tax collectors. And because He did, these people were changed. As Christ's representatives in our neighborhoods, we can allow God to make His appeal through us.

The Art of Small Talk

You should make small talk your major ministry. You need to be willing to give yourself to people where they are, in the ordinary tasks of living. Small talk is the natural language of everyday lives. You should learn to enjoy those brief encounters with your neighbors.

You should be careful, though, not to have a hidden agenda of giving a canned gospel presentation. You're not trying to make something happen; you're trying to be a part of what is happening without manipulating relationships.

Your neighbors ought to be able to relax with you, to get to know that they can trust you. They need to see that you are interested in them as people, not as just another potential notch in your Bible.

Often when I see one of my neighbors out in front, getting the mail or doing some yard work, I'll go over and strike up a conversation. In a minute or two, someone else will come over. Pretty soon we'll have several people there chatting and getting to know one another better.

Most people want relationships and a sense of community with their neighbors, but they're not sure how to go about it. When they see it happening, they're eager to join in. As a Christian in your neighborhood, you can reach out to others and set the example by being a good listener and making time for people to talk with you.

Becoming a Part of Their Lives

Most of your neighbors' lives are not lived in crisis, but in the ordinary. Learning the art of small talk will help you to become a part of their ordinary lives. If you can become a significant part of their ordinary lives, when crisis comes, you will be invited in there, too.

It was during normal small talk that the woman down the block let us know about her life-threatening illness. She let us in because we had taken the time to get to know her.

Recently a younger couple experienced a sudden layoff from work. We had talked with them on several occasions and had shared an evening with them. When I found out about the layoff, I felt comfortable asking about their finances, and they felt comfortable being honest.

We arranged a gift from our church deacons fund to help them when their rent was due. Within a month he found work through an interview with a plant manager who was a member of our church. Their family started coming to church regularly.

It is easy to make small talk. Careers and kids are good topics. Hobbies, sports, family activities, current events, positive aspects of the neighborhood, property items (cars, boats, pets, gardens, houses, furniture, appliances, etc.), home improvement projects, books, films, nearby eating places, where they lived before, and even religious topics are all great discussion starters.

The most important element is being willing to take the time to be with neighbors. Show them that it's important for you to talk with them and find out more about them.

Create Opportunities

Be generous about having neighbors in for a meal or over for a barbecue. Each time you invite a family, you are saying that you want to get to know them. Invite more than one family over to encourage them to get to know each other better. The key is simple meals that help everyone to be comfortable and to know that they can have you and others over without making it a costly affair.

Keep your eye open for opportunities to do things together with your neighbors. It may be a shared interest in sports, a hobby, or certain family outings. Inviting a neighbor to go fishing or hiking could open up a lasting relationship.

If you have a video recorder, you might have a family movie in your home and invite families in. I've known couples who have had a good response to parenting discussions in their homes. And if the opportunity presents itself, the neighborhood Bible study is still the most effective way to bring truth into the lives of your neighbors.

Judie and I both try to meet new neighbors quickly. On moving day we like to take them something, a pitcher of iced tea or a casserole for their evening meal. We also try to invite new neighbors over quickly. The longer you wait, the higher it seems the walls go up. When you meet new neighbors, work hard on getting their names and using them each time you see them.

It all comes back to the art of small talk. During the times of sharing the everyday aspects of life, you will hear needs that can become open doors to ministering the practical love of Christ.

Ministering Practical Love

Another important way to be Christ's ambassadors to your neighbors is to take opportunities to care for them in practical, down-to-earth ways.

A young woman I was counseling told me that several Christian families lived in the neighborhood where she grew up. She remembers the many winter mornings when it had snowed during the night and her family would get up to find their sidewalk and driveway already shoveled. No one would know which Christian family had done it.

Or her family would go away for vacations and come home to find that their lawn had been watered and mowed and their vegetable and flower garden weeded. She said this kind of practical, loving action was a major reason she always knew that Christianity was true.

Keep your eyes open for little ways you can have the same effect. Don't push yourself on others, but watch for opportunities for when your help is really needed.

For men it might be helping to carry in a heavy appliance, lending a hand on a project that's difficult to handle alone, or giving advice on mechanics or electrical work. For women it is often emergency baby-sitting or providing meals when another mom is sick. These are all practical ways we can love our neighbors.

Pets and Kids

Loving your neighbors' kids and pets can open doors to a deeper relationship. Are you willing to take care of your neighbors' pets while they're away? Though it's usually easy to do, it means a great deal to the family.

Consider inviting one of the neighbor kids along when you go for ice cream, to the pool, fishing, or to some sporting event. Your kids should feel free to ask friends along to Sunday School. This is another way that families can come into contact with church life and the love of Christ.

My own three boys love to play football. We seldom play a game anymore without having a number of the neighbor kids join in. We've even moved our games from the backyard to the front to be more accessible to the neighbors.

Staying Put

It takes time for relationships to grow and for love to make its way into people's hearts. If you give your neighborhood time, you will see good things happen. By choosing to stay put, you can swim against the current of upward mobility and say something important about your commitment to people.

When Judie and I considered our move, nothing major had begun to happen in our neighborhood. But there were some good signs. We decided that if we moved, it would be like a gardener preparing the soil, planting the seed, watering and cultivating the plants, and then abandoning the garden just before harvest time.

With work we can become the aroma of Christ to our neighbors. If we are dedicated to laying down our lives in service to others, sensitive to their personal needs, and engaged in meeting them with second-mile loving, we will influence our neighborhoods for Christ.

Taken from *Everyday Evangelism*, by Tom Eisenman, copyright 1987 by Inter-Varsity Christian Fellowship of the U.S.A., and used by permission of InterVarsity Press, P.O. Box 1400, Downers Grove, IL 60515.

Other Dialog Series Books

Building Self-esteem

The Christian and Money Management

Christian Personality Under Construction

Christians in a Crooked World

Coping with Traumas of Family Life

How to Improve Your Prayer Life

How to Live the Holy Life

Life Issues That Can't Be Ignored

No Easy Answers: Christians Debate Today's Issues

Questions You Shouldn't Ask About Christianity

Questions You Shouldn't Ask About the Church

Timeless Truths for Timely Living

Tough Questions—Christian Answers

What Jesus Said About . . .

When Life Gets Rough

For a discription of all available Dialog Series books, including some that may not be listed here, contact your local bookstore or your publishing house and ask for the free Dialog Series brochure.